Tempo: A Scarecrow Press Music Series on Rock, Pop, and Culture

Series Editor: Scott Calhoun

Tempo: A Scarecrow Press Music Series of Rock, Pop, and Culture offers titles that explore rock and popular music through the lens of social and cultural history, revealing the dynamic relationship between musicians, music, and their milieu. Like other major art forms, rock and pop music comment on their cultural, political, and even economic situation, reflecting the technological advances, psychological concerns, religious feelings, and artistic trends of their times. Contributions to the Tempo series are the ideal introduction to major pop and rock artists and genres.

Titles in the Series

BON JOVI

America's Ultimate Band

Margaret Olson

THE SCARECROW PRESS, INC.
Lanham • Toronto • Plymouth, UK
2013

Published by Scarecrow Press, Inc.
A wholly owned subsidiary of The Rowman & Littlefield Publishing Group, Inc.
4501 Forbes Boulevard, Suite 200, Lanham, Maryland 20706
www.rowman.com

10 Thornbury Road, Plymouth PL6 7PP, United Kingdom

British Library Cataloguing in Publication Information Available

Library of Congress Cataloging-in-Publication Data

Olson, Margaret, 1971–
Bon Jovi : America's ultimate band / Margaret Olson.
pages cm. — (Tempo: a Scarecrow Press music series on rock, pop, and culture)
Includes bibliographical references and index.
ISBN 978-0-8108-8661-2 (cloth : alk. paper) — ISBN 978-0-8108-8662-9 (ebook)
1. Bon Jovi (Musical group) 2. Rock musicians—United States—Biography. I. Title.
ML421.B68O47 2013
782.42166092'2—dc23
[B] 2013013754

♾™ The paper used in this publication meets the minimum requirements of American National Standard for Information Sciences Permanence of Paper for Printed Library Materials, ANSI/NISO Z39.48-1992.

Printed in the United States of America.

All photographs in the book (between chapter 3 and chapter 4) by Sherry Frank.

CONTENTS

FOREWORD

Bon Jovi is now so enmeshed in American popular culture it seems as if the band has been around forever, always ready to go: on the radio, on the jukebox, on a summer concert stage, or on a benefit television show. There is an ease and pleasure to much of their music that belies their skill, professionalism, and honorable pursuits, much like the post–Vietnam War suburban American way of life that has embraced them and given them the commercial success only a few second-gener-ation rock bands can claim. Fans not looking for an argument quickly warmed to Bon Jovi in the early 1980s. Many of those fans sought release from and validation for their workaday life, and they enjoyed cheering for more glamorous versions of themselves. Bon Jovi drew male and female crowds from the beginning, though their career path has been paved more abundantly by women in the audience.

If there could be a simple way to explain Bon Jovi's appeal to men and women, it would be that men find in Bon Jovi a strong backbone, both of defiance and for defending the weak and vulnerable, as well as permission to put down their fists once in a while and enjoy the party; women find in Bon Jovi men who can do just that: stand on their own, fight for what's right, and then dance the night away (hopefully right into the bedroom). But such a reductive explanation, tempting as it is, demeans both the band and its fans if it dismisses other essential desires and accomplishments that are part of the Bon Jovi equation.

Bon Jovi is an aspirational effect and affect of American culture. Men and women who listen to the band hear validation as well as inspiration for the "middle American" of modest means with noble dreams. At a Bon Jovi show, fans relax in the presence of a like-minded community. It is as if the most successful (and beautiful) men on the block were throwing a backyard party for the whole neighborhood and the invitation read "come as you are."

In this respect, their songs reinforce American themes: taking charge of one's own life, persevering through trials, finding dignity in work, drawing strength from family and community, and enjoying the spoils of victory. Bon Jovi did not bring a punk ethic or look; there was no Eurostyle; and they had, at best, a loose relationship with the conspicuous performativity of the Hair Band phenomenon, which placed a premium on personal appearance and stage spectacle. Bon Jovi was a product of the Jersey Shore of the 1970s and took its cues from the region's history of show bands plying their trade in want of steady work in front of mixed-gender audiences. From Asbury Park to New York City, like-minded bands raised the stakes of the profession by privileging musicianship as much as showmanship. So, while each band member was proficient on his instrument to begin with, each was also motivated to develop and refine his skill to keep him on top.

Bon Jovi—like the best bands—was supremely competitive, its sights set on beating out the competition by playing ever larger concert halls. Those bigger stages were, for the most part, outside the Philly–New Jersey–New York City circuit. West of the Jersey Shore lay country music and the blues, and while no one would mistake Bon Jovi for either of those kinds of bands, the band picked up enough tints and tones from across middle America to broaden its appeal from coast to coast. Once it captured the attention of mainstream America, it was able to tour globally and offer international audiences a proud but non-threatening taste of dyed-in-the-wool red, white, and blue.

Bon Jovi's own aspirations combined with a practical intelligence for survival helped it slip out from specific cultural strangleholds of the 1980s. The friendships among the core members helped the band negotiate personal and professional challenges in the 1990s, and its embrace of marketing methods in a rapidly changing music industry has served it well to the present day. Bon Jovi is middle America's show band, yes, and can lay claim to being America's ultimate band, but it also has a conscience. In its songs and tours, one sees its roots in working-class culture and honest dialogue about the trials and joys of everyday life for millions of middle Americans. In performing for more than thirty years, Bon Jovi has become a part of American culture itself.

Scott Calhoun
Series Editor

TIMELINE

1983	Formation of Bon Jovi
1984	*Bon Jovi* released in United States
1984	Formation of fund-raising concert Band Aid
1985	*7800° Fahrenheit* released
1985	First annual MTV awards broadcast; introduction of the compact disc; "We Are the World" single released to support African victims of famine
1985	Bon Jovi performs at first Farm Aid relief concert
1985	Formation of the Parents Music Resource Center to increase awareness of violence, drugs, and sex in popular music
1986	*Slippery When Wet* released
1986–1989	Increasing presence and abuse of cocaine in the music industry
1987	Bon Jovi on the cover of *Rolling Stone*
1988	*New Jersey* released
1988	Doc McGhee pleads guilty to drug smuggling
1989	Jon Bon Jovi marries Dorothea Hurley
1992	*Keep the Faith* released

1993	Bon Jovi performs at the Moscow Music Peace Festival
1994	Bassist Alec John Such departs the band; Richie Sambora marries Heather Locklear
1995	*These Days* released
2000	*Crush* released; Bon Jovi receives first Grammy nomination for Best Rock Album
2000	Metallica vs. Napster court case
2001	September 11 terrorist attacks in United States
2003	Bon Jovi twentieth anniversary
2005	*Have a Nice Day* released
2005	Hurricane Katrina
2006	Jon Bon Jovi Soul Foundation established in Philadelphia, PA
2007	*Lost Highway* released
2008	*Lost Highway* highest-grossing tour of the year
2009	*The Circle* released; Jon Bon Jovi and Richie Sambora inducted into Songwriters Hall of Fame; *When We Were Beautiful* documentary premieres on Showtime
2010	*Bon Jovi's Greatest Hits: The Ultimate Collection* released
2010	David Bryan's musical *Memphis* wins American Theatre Wing Tony Award for Best Musical
2011	Richie Sambora temporarily leaves tour
2012	Jon Bon Jovi appointed to President Barack Obama's White House Council for Community Solutions
2013	*What Happens Now* released
2013	Richie Sambora temporarily leaves tour (April)

ACKNOWLEDGMENTS

I would like to thank Scarecrow Press, specifically Bennett Graff and Scott Calhoun, for creating a series to explore the meaning of music in culture and culture in music. Thank you to Elizabeth S. Olson for your assistance. Thank you to Sherry A. Frank for making the trek to New Jersey to take the beautiful photos used in the book. Thank you to Ed Jankowski, Lari Dempsey, Al Fetterer, David Ferrari, and all the individuals who participated in the polls and surveys. Let me tender a very special thank you to Stephanie Ward and Sherry Frank for their tireless efforts in conducting polls and surveys under often embarrassing conditions and for their exhaustive support of all things "Bon Jovi." I would like to offer a special thank you to Marilynn and Michael S. Olson. Thank you to the British Library Music Reference Series and libraries at the University of Chicago. Thank you to Beth M. Gulewich and Michael Brian Martin, faculty at Broughton High School, Raleigh, North Carolina, for their assistance. And, finally, thank you to Jon, Richie, Tico, and David. We're all just livin' on a prayer.

INTRODUCTION

When thinking of the relationship between musical artists and their wider cultural context, there may be no better example than Bon Jovi of a band ingrained in American and world culture. This self-described all-American band of brothers from New Jersey has played music together for over thirty years. Along the way they have toured the globe, broken through international barriers by performing in dozens of countries, defined MTV in the 1980s, sold over 130 million records, collected numerous awards, gained a loyal multigenerational fan base along the way, contributed to 9/11 relief work, and set a new standard in American philanthropy.

Bon Jovi is a uniquely American story. Jon Bon Jovi, Richie Sambora, Tico Torres, and David Bryan come from the same part of the country; in fact, three of them were delivered by the same doctor in the same hospital. They exhibit a set of, for lack of a better term, old-school values: unyielding ambition, a tireless work ethic, a dyed-in-the-wool kind of professionalism, and a real sense of gratitude.

When they started by playing tiny clubs on the Jersey Shore, the odds of making it big were set well against them—and yet they overcame each obstacle in their path to stardom through sheer determination and the tenacity of the band leader, Jon Bon Jovi. After the seemingly requisite crisis period in the early 1990s—the firing of their manager and original bass player—the band regrouped and has never looked back.

My personal interest in the band dates to the golden days of MTV in the 1980s. Their best-known song, "Livin' on a Prayer," epitomized MTV. It stood as middle-of-the-road rock and yet it was so much more: it was a stadium anthem that served as the centerpiece during the infancy of the music television channel that would change music itself. The stage pyrotechnics, the larger-than-life hair and clothes, and the group's overwhelming energy immediately caught my attention. However, like many Generation Xers, I, too, would part ways from Bon Jovi for a number of years. It was while attending a *Lost Highway* concert in 2008 that what I found more fascinating than what was happening on-stage was what was happening in the audience itself. While men certainly were in attendance, the audience struck me as overwhelmingly female. Moreover, many of the women were of a certain age and appeared to represent every socioeconomic stratum. I had to wonder: What motivated these women, with career and family responsibilities, no doubt, to buy a ticket to a rock concert in the middle of the week? The answer was pretty simple: Jon Bon Jovi. Women love this guy.

The whole concert experience raised many questions. Are all the fans at concerts the original fans from the '80s? Where were the men? How did Bon Jovi survive where most other bands formed in the '80s faded into the background? How can a band prove so popular despite its lack of acceptance by established media critics? In short, why do people love this band?

These questions, and others, became the impetus for this volume in the Tempo series. It should be noted at the outset that this "cultural" biography and analysis of the band was written without the cooperation or endorsement of Bon Jovi. My examination is more outside looking in, drawing heavily on printed sources, radio and television interviews, fan responses, and the 2010 documentary film *When We Were Beautiful*. There are clear limits in not having the cooperation of the subject. But there are benefits, too. This assessment is not so much what Bon Jovi was—or thinks it was—as what Bon Jovi *means* given its continued prominence as one of America's few remaining "super band" acts. In that regard, Bon Jovi as one of the last standing arena rock bands may well be America's ultimate band.

The first two chapters provide basic historical context with data on the formation of Bon Jovi, the band members' early years, and an overview of the band's discography. The third chapter, "MTV's Band for a

Generation," explores the connection between Bon Jovi and the original music channel, MTV, with looks at roles played by Bon Jovi's iconic music videos in music history and their place alongside the videos of the other prominent artists featured on the channel at that time.

The fourth chapter considers the influence of drugs and the subsequent sobriety on the band, folding in the difficulties raised by Bon Jovi's original manager's drug smuggling operation, all of which eventually led to Jon Bon Jovi's anti-drug outreach activities in order to stay out of prison and on the road. The fifth chapter, "Cross-Commercialism as a Survival Tool," discusses the band's many commercial outlets and how their various business interests have kept the band relevant through the years.

Chapter six considers the extent to which gender plays a role both in maintaining a fan base and in the operation of the Bon Jovi organization. It questions why the quality of the music of the band was considered secondary to their looks by critics. It also explores the long-term marriage of Jon Bon Jovi to Dorothea Hurley and the effect that has had on the band's longevity and credibility with female fans. The Bon Jovi brand, in turn, becomes the focus of chapter seven, exploring the marketing of Bon Jovi as a concept and the band's realization of the golden nugget that is brand recognition. The eighth chapter looks at the philanthropic work of the band, specifically Jon Bon Jovi and his significant work as a political activist for the issues of homelessness and poverty, as well as his relationships with current politicians.

If you know nothing about Bon Jovi the book may inspire you to listen to their music. If you are a longtime fan of the band, the book may offer something about the band you did not already know. If you are interested in music's place in modern American culture, you may identify with parallels drawn in the book.

Bon Jovi has survived and thrived over a long career of change and growth and contributed significantly to society. It cannot be denied that the band has been unapologetically present and fully engaged in American life: no small thing for any major act today.

I

AN AMERICAN BAND

ASBURY PARK, NEW JERSEY

Bon Jovi does not exist without New Jersey. In order to understand the band, it is useful to know something about the music culture of Asbury Park, New Jersey. Throughout the early 20th century Asbury Park flourished as a seaside resort, but with the construction of the Garden State Parkway in the mid-century and the development of shopping malls outside city limits, tourists began to go elsewhere. It is hard to imagine now, but before there was Atlantic City, there was Asbury Park. In the 1960s there was increasing social tension, and the year 1970 brought severe race riots to Asbury Park. Buildings and businesses were burned and destroyed, and those events marked the beginning of the end for the thriving business and tourism community. In recent years, there has been a strong movement to revitalize and restore the town to its former glory. The fact that Asbury Park developed a thriving and vital music community and culture all its own makes the ragged history of this tiny part of the Jersey Shore more than noteworthy.

Building on the music tradition of bandstand performances that took place on the Boardwalk in older days, Asbury Park musicians were able to create a close-knit community that supported each other personally and professionally. These accomplished musicians also created and performed a great deal of original music. Jon Bon Jovi remembers those days:

I gotta tell you, it was a time . . . there [was] a great camaraderie amongst players and musicians and songwriters . . . back in 1980, '81, '82, '83 back in Asbury, the scene was perhaps past its prime, but the sheen hadn't exactly worn off yet. There was still this kind of "who's next, who's the next guy to come out of here?" And the support system was there, and the idea that you could still reach that crazy dream of making a record someday was still alive and well. And we were so young. That had something to do with it.[1]

The Asbury Park music culture produced many diverse American bands like The Smithereens, Dramarama, Steel Mill, Cats, In Between Dreams, and Red House. Southside Johnny and the Asbury Jukes stand alone as the ultimate house band that personified the "Asbury sound" of hard rhythm and blues rock. Bruce Springsteen and his E Street Band remain the heart and soul of the Asbury Park music scene. Jon himself recalls Bruce's far-reaching legendary status: "I used to walk the Boardwalk when I was fifteen years old, expecting Bruce to be just standing there, sort of like a statue."[2]

Because of the Shore's central location between New York City and Philadelphia and the tourism market in those years, musicians were able to play to live audiences and practice the art of live performance. Professional musicians could try out songs on audiences before taking their show on the road to Manhattan or Philly.

The Asbury Park sound is generally described as all-American rhythm-and-blues-infused rock. Musicians who have been part of the Asbury scene may agree that there are similar musical attributes among the bands; however, most prefer to think of themselves as influenced by rather than imitative of other Asbury Park musicians. Asbury musician Tony Amato offers his opinion: "Asbury sound . . . what Asbury sound? There is no way that the Shakes sound any way like the Jukes. The Jukes don't sound anything like Cahoots. Cahoots don't sound anything like the E Street Band."[3] In reality, there have been music trends among the Asbury artists (for example, the brass sections of the Asbury Jukes and E Street Band), but no *one* group can own a sound or summarize a truly diverse community of artists.

According to the legendary Asbury musician Southside Johnny, the music scene is generally thought to have peaked in the decade of 1969–1979, and the music that followed this time was a dim reflection of the glory days. The release of Bruce Springsteen's *Born to Run* in

1975 made Asbury Park extremely relevant to record companies. Industry executives made the trip out from Manhattan to find the next New Jersey music genius. Audiences and critics alike were interested again in what was happening in that area. All of this attention resulted in a creative musical era on the Shore.

Asbury Park was a place where Bruce Springsteen would jump onstage and jam with an unknown band, and where the Jukes would call a young, inexperienced Jon Bon Jovi onstage to sing a number with the pros. Exciting things were happening at watering holes like the Stone Pony and the FastLane. It is hard to imagine now, but in the day, Asbury Park was heaven on earth for young people interested in rock and roll and the musicians that wanted to play for them. Kids could go to the Boardwalk area and have their pick of clubs where they could stumble upon great music any given night. For young musicians in New Jersey, it was like having a rock and blues training ground in their backyard. For the young Jon Bon Jovi it was proof that a New Jersey musician could make it big, very big.

There is no question that the music culture of Asbury Park had a singular influence on Jon Bon Jovi as a musician. The appealing combination of professional musicians doing their thing and brotherly camaraderie would have been irresistible to a comer like Bon Jovi. Jon was not the only band member influenced by Bruce Springsteen. Drummer Tico Torres remembers those days: "Growing up with Bruce when he was still unknown, it was like seeing how the music developed, and his type of music actually set a tone for a lot of other musicians to follow. To be a part of that . . . I think the best way to put it is, that was an honor."[4] Keyboardist David Bryan also recalls: "Springsteen was the lord of Asbury Park when Jon and I were in high school, and it was just neat to see him come down to the club, and now we're a peer."[5]

It didn't hurt that Bruce Springsteen's *Born to Run* defined a new season of American rock. When the album was released Jon was thirteen years old and studying guitar. He had a direct connection to one of the top rock albums in the country at the time and understood the cultural themes of the songs in an organic way. He was able to experience that music firsthand, know and understand where it originated, and see it gain national attention from his own home. This hometown connection exerted a profound influence on Jon Bon Jovi and other young musicians and their psyches as they considered what was possible for themselves. The music culture of Asbury Park contributed in no small way to the creation of Bon Jovi; as Jon put it: "It's hard to sum it up in one sound bite. The truth of it is . . . my teeth were cut in Asbury Park, New Jersey, in 1980."[6]

THE BEGINNING

The evolution of Bon Jovi began when Jon's family, the Bongiovis, moved to Sayreville, New Jersey, and Jon started attending Sayreville High School. There he met several friends who were also interested in music. They decided to put together an authentic rhythm and blues band (playing rhythm and blues was probably not a typical activity of high school students). The group eventually settled into a ten-piece rhythm and blues band known as Atlantic City Expressway (ACE) in 1979. Two young men Jon knew from the Jersey music scene, David Bryan Rashbaum (who would go by David Bryan) and Dave Sabo, were invited to join the group on keyboard and guitar, respectively.

From all accounts, Atlantic City Expressway was successful for a group of high school guys with no professional experience. The band focused on covering tunes and not on creating original music. They played at clubs on the Jersey Shore, and even though they were underage, they had a devoted following of family and friends who came to shows.

Eventually ACE disbanded and Jon found his way to a smaller group known as The Rest, which had regular gigs on the Shore, opening for Southside Johnny and other national acts at clubs like the FastLane. It was a short-lived stay for their new lead singer. Around this time, Jon started other temporary groups, such as The Lechers and The Wild Ones. When he finally set his sights on becoming a professional musician, he reached out to a friend of his father's. A cousin of the family, Tony Bongiovi, owned a popular recording studio in New York City known as the Power Station and hired Jon for an entry-level job at the studio. He worked hard at menial tasks such as sweeping and running errands, and also had extraordinary opportunities to interact with professional musicians and recording artists. Aerosmith, the Talking Heads, the Ramones, and Huey Lewis and the News were just a few of the groups recording at the Station in those days. He was allowed to record demo tracks after hours, when the professional artists had finished for the night. One of these sessions led to a studio recording of Jon's original song, "Runaway," backed by professional studio musicians including bassist Hugh McDonald, who still collaborates with Bon Jovi to this day.

THE DEVELOPMENT OF THE BAND

Never one to wait for something to happen, once Bon Jovi had his "Runaway" demo ready, he set about finding management. Colleagues from the Power Station worked the New York angle, specifically the radio station WAPP, to get the record played. Jon and David Bryan took a trip to the West Coast to personally shop the record around Los Angeles. The hard work and determination was eventually rewarded. After someone at WAPP recognized the potential of "Runaway," it started to gain some serious airplay. Jon Bon Jovi then set to work putting together his permanent band, which included David Bryan (keyboards), Tico Torres (drums), Dave Sabo (guitar), and Alec John Such (bass). They started playing together at clubs up and down the Jersey Shore. When "Runaway" proved a success, the management companies came calling, and Jon Bon Jovi signed a deal with Polygram Records as a solo artist. At some point during this transitional period (the only real one in the band's history), an acquaintance of Tico Torres and Alec John Such came to replace Dave Sabo as lead guitarist. His name was Richie Sambora.

Bon Jovi now consisted of native New Jerseyites and New Yorkers: John Francis Bongiovi Jr., b. 1962, from Perth Amboy, New Jersey; Richard Stephen Sambora, b. 1959, from Woodbridge, New Jersey; David Bryan Rashbaum, b. 1962, from Edison, New Jersey; Hector "Tico" Torres, b. 1952, from New York City; and Alec John Such, b. 1956, from Yonkers, New York. All of the members of the band were working as professional musicians before Bon Jovi.

The specific details aside, sometime after this group was put together, the record deal at Polygram was most likely amended from representing Jon Bon Jovi as an individual artist to representing the band as a unit. Whatever the terms of the management agreement, the choice of band name was Bon Jovi. Other possible names for the band that were briefly considered were Victory and Johnny Lightning. It has been said that the reason the parties involved decided to use Bon Jovi as the band's name is because Jon had already released a single for a compilation album under this name. It seemed like a logical business decision for the young band. Another view is that Jon considered himself the lead band member in all things and was determined to succeed or fail under his own name. Whatever the reason, Bon Jovi was incorporated in 1983.

Around this time, Jon became acquainted with music manager Doc McGhee and was impressed by his work with the new Los Angeles club band Mötley Crüe. Bon Jovi eventually signed him as the band's manager. Within the span of a few months, Doc McGhee had them touring as the opening act for the Scorpions, Ratt, and Kiss in the United States and Europe. From most accounts Bon Jovi had successful personal and professional relationships with the bands on tour.

THE FIRST ALBUM: *BON JOVI*

The world culture of popular music in 1984 was nothing if not diverse. Soft rock was represented by Madonna and Phil Collins, new wave British music by The Police and New Order, and heavy metal by Ozzy Osbourne, Metallica, and Black Sabbath. This would be the year Van Halen released one of their most successful albums, titled *1984.* Duran Duran, Wham!, Billy Joel, Prince, and Tina Turner all had hit records.

This was the environment in which Bon Jovi released their eponymous debut album in 1984. Original songwriting and powerful energy on the album immediately presented Bon Jovi as a serious band. Their name, cover art, lyrics, and the mood of the album offered an original band to the listening public. The first album may not have launched any number one songs, but it did reveal a band actively searching for their own unique sound and identity. The album became the foundation of one of the longest band histories in American popular music.

Bon Jovi had rehearsed and played enough together in live performance that they were already cohesive as a musical group at the time *Bon Jovi* was released in 1984. Their unity brought a confidence and maturity to the material that most young bands did not possess at the time. The participation of Tico "The Hit Man" Torres, a seasoned and slightly older musician, also made a great contribution to the band's overall level of professionalism.

These were not musicians for hire, but songwriters who had the plan of a long-term career in mind from the very beginning. There can be no doubt, as evidenced by his subsequent success, that Jon Bon Jovi has always been a serious businessman. Whether owing to his exposure to seasoned musicians on the Jersey Shore, the professional artists he observed at the Power Station, or the ideals ingrained by his parents, he understood the value of creating and producing his own music, rather than existing as a product of a record or publishing company. Bon Jovi knew that you had to write your own music to have optimum staying power.

Musically, Bon Jovi makes a strong statement. First and foremost, Jon's voice stands out as one of strength and quality. His voice is very pleasant without being weak or understated, attractive without being feminine, and able to provide roughness when it is demanded by the lyrics or music. Jon has the natural ability to emphasize certain words in order to bring across an emotion or thought to his audience. He also earns much credit for actually articulating the lyrics in such a way that they can be clearly understood, a rare trait in rock that he has continued throughout his career. Richie Sambora's gifts are also clearly evident on this album. Even though he was not part of the recording of "Runaway," he makes his mark on the other tunes. When it comes to Sambora, there is no warming up into a guitar solo. He simply attacks it with cold precision from the moment he starts playing; in addition, his significant contributions as a songwriter help make the album work. Tico Torres brings more years of experience to the band than the other members, and this is most evident in the strong, unyielding anchor of support he provides throughout the album. He is a musician who clearly knows when to push forward and when to allow others to stand out. On this album, he holds the band together rhythmically. David Bryan also brings songwriting skills to material on the album, as well as a sense of drama with his keyboard skills. Even on this first album, he is already experimenting with different keyboard instruments and his signature keyboard/organ/piano introductions.

The overwhelming theme of this record is "the man who has been done wrong by his woman," which is offered in several permutations, including the girl who cheats on her man; the girl who takes off with another man (prompting a vengeance killing); and the woman who wants her ex-man to leave her alone. There is no question that the lyrics are from an exclusively male perspective; however, while yearning for and fighting with women may come across as a rather one-dimensional theme for a record, the band earns credit for consistency and commitment.

There is an unevenness to the songs on the album, but there are a few standouts. "Runaway" has the distinction of being the original Bon Jovi song. Ironically, it was not recorded by the current members of Bon Jovi, only with Jon and Hugh McDonald. The relentless keyboard motif drives the idea of running away throughout the song. The dead-solid percussion provides a strong support and brings a sense of urgency and pacing. There is just enough of a rough edge to the instrumentation to cross that line from pop to metal. The vocal harmonies are subtle but effective, and the high vocal descant at the very end of the song is memorable. The a cappella section, "she's a little runaway," makes the harmonies pop in the middle of the song and is an effective surprise. This song, in addition to "She Don't Know Me," is Jon's most accomplished song on the album, mainly because of his integrated use of lyric and emotion within the vocal line.

"Roulette" is significant because it is the first published songwriting collaboration between Jon and Richie Sambora. For a first effort, it is a cohesive offering that deals with the subject matter of love as a game and the love triangle ("I need you, you want him"). The songwriters are clear in their song form from this first offering onward. The typical Bon Jovi song form of introduction, verse, chorus, bridge, guitar solo, partial verse, and chorus that makes up "Roulette" will be repeated in the future. The title of the piece, the use of text to elicit the game in motion (red, black, spinning), create a unity of theme that simply works. Musically, there is unexpected rhythmic variation that can catch the listener off guard but ultimately creates another layer of interest. Richie Sambora's technically tight guitar introduction delivers all the necessary squeaks and squeals to give the piece the bite it needs. He creates a very fierce guitar riff that is both in your face and easy to listen to, an interesting artistic combination.

"She Don't Know Me" is the one song on the album that Jon did not have a hand in composing. The lyrics and tune were written by Mark Avsec in 1980, and it is clearly identifiable as an '80s song. The call-and-response approach is used cleverly here, although there is a great deal of repetition too. There is also a long interlude that seems an ill fit for the song, and Jon sings another high descant at the end of the piece, reminiscent of "Runaway," though much more subdued. It is ironic that Jon seems to have more of a feel for the lyrics for this song, which he did not write, than for his own songs. His delivery of the melodic lines in "She Don't Know Me" is more cohesive overall than on the album's other songs.

"Shot through the Heart" reveals Jon's sophisticated understanding of how to vocally shape the lyrics to reflect an emotion or textual concept. Even from this first album, he is able to deliver a melodic line that makes sense emotionally and musically. The piece really picks up on the guitar solo; again, Richie Sambora can rip into it right from the top of the solo and demonstrates skill far beyond his years. David Bryan's arpeggiated chords of the piano part create a questioning atmosphere. An instrumental piano and guitar duet prior to the bridge complement each other to good effect. Random cries of "Shot! Shot!" give the piece extra energy. There is an arrogant and charming chuckle in the middle of the song. The song title, "Shot through the Heart," is the first time we associate Bon Jovi with the word "shot," which is also sprinkled throughout the album. The band would borrow from itself with this title later in the band's career as a line in the song "You Give Love a Bad Name."

Bon Jovi had introduced itself to the listening audience as a band that is not full of pretense or artifice. At their worst, the lyrics can be interpreted as one-dimensional, but at their best they are strong in their personal truth and singleness of mind.

THE FIRST VIDEO: "RUNAWAY"

With the debut of MTV (Music TeleVision) in 1981 came the dawn of the music video, and the music industry changed the way music was distributed and marketed forever. There was now an expectation from the music industry that industry-represented bands would create music videos to promote their music. In the '80s, teenagers were planning their Friday and Saturday nights around the debut of the latest music video on MTV, and bands had to deliver.

The release of Bon Jovi's debut album in 1984 practically required them to release videos of their popular singles to help gain an audience and raise their profile. Their first video of the song "Runaway" started a tradition of general dislike by the band of the whole process of video making. It would not be until well into their career that the band would be satisfied with a Bon Jovi video.

This core group of musicians appeared together in the first Bon Jovi video, "Runaway," but they did not participate in the original recording of the song. Jon said: "They were on the first album, but they weren't on 'Runaway' or those demo tapes. I put the band together about two months before I had a deal, when 'Runaway' was on the radio and breaking nationally. The band in the video is my band, but it's not the band that recorded the song."[7]

The director of the "Runaway" video, Robert Mont, claimed that the Stephen King novel *Firestarter* was the reference for the video.[8] The four-minute-and-sixteen-second video features images of fire, interspersed with close-ups of a girl running away from her parents and Bon Jovi rocking out. The images don't really reflect the intent or style of the band. Jon Bon Jovi remembers his first video experience: "I mean I sat with these guys [from Polygram Records] telling me I should be singing on the White Cliffs of Dover, and these other guys telling me I should be a swashbuckler and riding horseback . . . this isn't what we're about."[9]

Jon learned from this experience and took more creative control over the image of the band in all aspects of advertising. In 1984, videos were an advertisement, essentially a commercial for the album, and artists cared about how they were portrayed. Other videos produced in 1984 convey the style of early music-video production: blatantly oversimplified story lines, flat production values, and less than polished hair and wardrobe. Artists of this time were still figuring out how to translate their music to the video experience. The music video format had not yet reached the sophistication level of short films that it eventually would with videos like Michael Jackson's "Thriller."

A classic American video during the year 1984 was Madonna's "Borderline." The plot is simple: a photographer discovers Madonna on the street, takes her picture, and makes her a star. The video has an urban home-video feel. The fashions of the day are reflected in Madonna's ripped stonewashed jean vest, red scarf tied into a bow around her head, and black lace fingerless gloves. Ratt's "Round and Round" from the same year gives the audience a macabre dinner party starring Milton Berle dressed in drag. The camera cuts from the dining room table to Ratt jamming out one floor above. The butler brings in a serving tray and removes the lid: rats for dinner. While imaginative in some respects, the video comes off as blatantly campy.

Bon Jovi did not take much inspiration from the music videos that already existed. They were also in the precarious position of being a brand-new band with no prior video-making experience and were required to listen to the input of the record company executives. While Jon was not yet in a position to take complete creative control of the band, these early experiences helped him to quickly realize that creative control was extremely important to him.

THE HAIR BAND COMPARISON

In the 1980s, the terms "hair band" and "glam metal" described a band that appeared to focus more on elaborate hairstyles and outlandish fashion than music. Warrant, Dokken, Winger, Guns N' Roses, Queensryche, Whitesnake, Mötley Crüe, Poison, and Bon Jovi were all loosely grouped into this limited and muddled category in the '80s. These bands actually represent subtle permutations of the metal, glam, and hair band genres prevalent in the '80s.

The early style of Bon Jovi reflects the fashion of the time. They were not as wild as Ratt and not polished European-cool like Depeche Mode. It was not until the mid-1990s that Bon Jovi hit their style stride. (There is a direct correlation between the more assured music of their 1992 album *Keep the Faith* and the maturing look of the band.) Critics like Ken Tucker had specific opinions: "In sound and appearance, the group is obviously heavily influenced by the reigning heroes of heavy metal, Van Halen."[10] Maybe not entirely a fair comparison? In 1984, Van Halen favored bright colors and animal prints. Eddie Van Halen never met a stripe he didn't like. Bon Jovi, in 1984, wore more solid, darker patterns, with black as the featured color.

The men of Bon Jovi have always garnered massive criticism for their "hair band" appearance. Those first opinions and viewpoints of the music critics in the '80s have stuck with the band to the present day and have most likely negatively affected the professional criticism of their body of work. The overall perception was that Bon Jovi's look was just not scary enough to produce real metal. Jon recalled the early days of trying to discover the band's authentic style: "In the early days we were still trying to find ourselves . . . we were from New Jersey, all we ever had was a pair of jeans and a leather jacket."[11] He went on to describe how the L.A. bands like Mötley Crüe and Ratt were doing something very different with fashion. He thought that the band needed to wear makeup and fake jewelry to make it big. He eventually realized it wasn't right for Bon Jovi: "It took a while to find ourselves, that's all. I mean, you walk down the street in Jersey wearing make-up, man, you're gonna get your ass kicked. So none of that stuff was really us."[12]

There can be no question that the looks of a band have an enormous effect on how the music of the band is interpreted. So in the case of Bon Jovi, if what the audience is hearing does not match what they are seeing, it could cause confusion. What music critics failed to recognize was that the classic American rock Bon Jovi played simply did not match the look of the band. Their music was more Bruce Springsteen, John Mellencamp, Bob Dylan, and totally original, but their look was more evocative of a group like Winger or Dokken. It took a few years, but Bon Jovi's looks finally matched up with their music.

For Bon Jovi, their hair band phase was only the first stage of their career, an awkward adolescence out of which they quickly grew. By wearing their hair long and teased, they were simply fitting into the style of the period. However, while their music did not exactly fit into any musical style, their early appearance did lean toward the hair band look. On the cover and insert of their first album, Bon Jovi is dressed quite simply for a hair band. They are wearing basic black with no makeup. Perhaps one reason their hair looks so good is that Jon's father, John Bongiovi Sr., was a professional hairstylist at the time. Even in their most outlandish fashion moment, Bon Jovi was never as feminine as Poison or Mötley Crüe. They simply never went that far.

Like any band that has had to reinvent itself in the interest of longevity, Bon Jovi has continued to change their look as individuals and as a band as their career progresses. While Bon Jovi's looks have always attracted a certain kind of attention, in reality they have always been a band that is music-focused and music-driven. The looks of the band are incidental to the musical quality and production.

CRITICS REACT TO BON JOVI

From the inception of Bon Jovi's career, the music critics have not been supportive. Even though Bon Jovi has never classified itself as a heavy metal band, the critics have constantly compared it to other heavy metal groups. An early example of a critic's reaction to Bon Jovi: "The group's debut album . . . is an assured if characterless synthesis of piercing guitar solos, arena-rock dynamics and big choruses . . . for all its guitar-bass-drums crunch, Bon Jovi has taken a step back from the unrepentant ferocity of heavy metal to a safer and more profitable territory."[13] Another example of a typical review in 1984: "Records from . . . Bon Jovi, Toto, Survivor, Echo and the Bunnymen . . . were generally awful—even though most of them got on the charts."[14]

In comparing the Bon Jovi debut album with the Scorpions or Mötley Crüe, the critics overlook the point that Bon Jovi is not heavy metal or "light" heavy metal. They are not pop or rock and roll. They are a hybrid of metal and hard rock. From a 1984 review: "Preceding the Scorpions will be Bon Jovi . . . below-average heavy metal, with an emphasis on the screeching vocals of its leader."[15] Throughout this early period, the critics failed to predict the future success of the band, as demonstrated in a review of a concert backing the Scorpions in 1984: "Opening act Bon Jovi is a young, New Jersey–based outfit led by singer-guitarist John [sic] Bon Jovi. Though the group's half-hour set demonstrated lots of youthful verve, it's hard to imagine anyone standing throughout one of its all-too-typical hard-rock workouts."[16]

Commercially, Bon Jovi's first album gained a solid foothold with the Billboard 100 top forty singles "Runaway" and "She Don't Know Me." The two singles were made into videos that were in heavy rotation on MTV and were the world's first look at the band.

EARLY TRAITS FOR SUCCESS

Why has Bon Jovi been able to achieve the kind of longevity in their career that many bands only dream about? There are probably several reasons, and many of them were early predictors of their eventual success. Perhaps the most important predictor of Bon Jovi's success was the fact that they were all skilled musicians. Unlike music "artists" who tend to have limited musical skills, each of the members of Bon Jovi knew his instrument and had skill and talent. They all have played more than one instrument in some capacity. David Bryan played piano well enough to attend Juilliard before dropping out to join Bon Jovi. Tico Torres was an accomplished studio musician with a good reputation and many album credits. Richie Sambora was gaining increasing attention for his guitar skills before joining Bon Jovi, having been invited to audition for Kiss. Alec John Such had worked professionally as a musician. Jon Bon Jovi could play guitar and sing very well.

All these elements combined to make a band that was very comfortable with live performance. They had all played in groups around the Jersey Shore, and after forming as a band were quickly heading out on national-level tours. They got their chops by playing live in clubs, arenas, concert halls, dives, and wherever else they could. The professional skills they honed in the early days gave them a strong foundation for the rest of their career.

Another predictor of success was the band's insistence on writing their own music. On the first album, three of the five band members contributed songs. Richie Sambora and Jon Bon Jovi came together as a songwriting team on the first album. Jon and David Bryan also collaborated on two songs on the first album. Original songwriting supported their commitment to finding an authentic sound.

Bon Jovi's willingness to do whatever it took and to work very hard is another reason they are still relevant today. Each has spoken plainly about his New Jersey work ethic. This work ethic is what drove the need of the band to gain live performing experience from the beginning. Hard work is what has kept several of the top mega-bands successful today. U2, the Rolling Stones, Metallica, AC/DC, and Bon Jovi, to name a few, all have to put the work into live performance, whether touring their first album or their twenty-first. With the practice of playing live and learning to handle anything thrown at them in public performance, Bon Jovi makes what they do on stage look easy. Perhaps this is one of the reasons they have been criticized. It just doesn't look hard enough.

BON JOVI'S SECRET WEAPON

The '70s and early '80s produced a plethora of heavy metal music. Mostly American and British bands flooded the global music market with screeching guitars and intense musical experiences. AC/DC, Ratt, and Quiet Riot were just a few of the metal bands making an impact during this time. It seems like the glam or light metal that followed this period was an organic reaction to the bands that preceded it—the relaxation of the contracted heavy metal muscle.

The climate for heavy metal was in flux during the early '80s. By that time, many subgenres of metal had made an appearance in American music: speed, death, thrash, black, glam, and extreme. There is one genre of metal missing from this list, which you will not find listed in any music encyclopedia: female-friendly metal.

Hard rock acts like AC/DC and Quiet Riot did not necessarily appeal to a cross-section of women, and this niche market was wide open for the right mix of metal and hard rock. Bon Jovi had something else on their side in that there was bound to be a backlash from the heavy metal that dominated the airwaves at the time. A lighter metal was the perfect thing. The genre was not too loud and weird, like Mötley Crüe, and not too gender confused, like Poison. It was not boys' hard rock either, dusty and dirty, and not at all pretty. It was fun, peppy, a little naughty, with a really cute lead singer. It was Bon Jovi.

The women's movement of the '70s was continuing to evolve, and young women were ready to take their place as rock and heavy metal fans. Both women and men were ready for a change. Their attitude was captured by Andy Secher, editor of *Hit Parader*: "They're sick and tired of Prince, the Thompson Twins, and Tears for Fears. It's real blue-collar . . . these kids want to party and get loose."[17] The fan base of young women who identified with Bon Jovi may well be Bon Jovi's secret weapon in their long career. Most of the women who attend Bon Jovi concerts today became fans in the mid-1980s.

2

THE SONGS

MUSICAL INFLUENCES

Bon Jovi is an American band that has been strongly influenced by both American and British rock. Individually and collectively, their music has been informed by the musicians who came before them. The band's early press clippings often contained suggestions that Bon Jovi was imitating a more musically inventive band. Van Halen was the most frequent suggestion. Bruce Springsteen and John Mellencamp were others. These comparisons have continued throughout their career. There can be no doubt that all the band members have personal musical influences that they have acknowledged over the years.

Tico Torres's influences include Elvin Jones, John Coltrane, Led Zeppelin, and the Beatles. Elvin Jones was an accomplished jazz drummer known for his innovative rhythmic techniques. In the 1960s he was a member of the John Coltrane Quartet, an experimental and improvisational group ahead of its time. Jones was a role model for Torres in that he was an arbiter of the complexities of rhythm. "Love's the Only Rule," from *The Circle*, includes a Coltrane tribute in the lyric "alive, like a lonely note from John Coltrane." John Bonham of Led Zeppelin is another influential drummer for Torres. Generally acknowledged as the most respected rock drummer of all time, he had a huge power in his playing and was known for making unusual and brilliant adjustments to the standard drum kit. He was also known for using extra large drumsticks, which undoubtedly added to his huge sound. Bonham's influence can be heard in Torres's musical style and as the rhythmic anchor for Bon Jovi. Bonham was a troubled but talented person, and he and Torres also shared the disease of alcoholism. Unfortunately, while Torres found sobriety through golf and art, Bonham died in 1980, of asphyxiation after drinking the equivalent of forty shots of vodka.

David Bryan's influences include Deep Purple, Led Zeppelin, Mozart, and Bach. As a classical pianist studying the great composers, he gained hard-won technical skills that enabled him to play any genre of music. As a musician, Bryan has much in common with Deep Purple's Jon Lord. While a keyboardist in the original heavy metal band, Deep Purple, Lord often used the Hammond organ. David Bryan has utilized this instrument as well. Both men were trained as classical pianists from an early age. Lord is known for his attempts to fuse the classical and rock genres in his playing. Bryan does this to a much lesser degree in his dramatic keyboard solo introductions like "Let It Rock"; however, he does infuse blues into rock when possible. Bryan's use of blues piano is clearly evident on the *Bon Jovi* album in "Get Ready" and in his independent composition work, like the Tony Award–winning musical *Memphis*. The musical style is reminiscent of Southside Johnny and the Asbury Jukes.

Richie Sambora's influences include Eric Clapton, Jimi Hendrix, Jeff Beck, and the Beatles. The influence of the Beatles permeates his songwriting, and he has mentioned them often as a seminal influence. His solo guitar playing continuously references the masters Clapton and Hendrix (Clapton was a guest artist on a track of Sambora's debut album, *Stranger in This Town*). Sambora acknowledges a special connection with the revolutionary playing of the Yardbirds' former guitarist Jeff Beck, whom he cites as a major musical influence. Beck's musical style of fusing heavy metal and jazz was ahead of his time, and influential on most rock guitarists that followed.

Jon Bon Jovi credits Southside Johnny and the Asbury Jukes, Bruce Springsteen, Bob Dylan, Thin Lizzy, Alice Cooper, and Aerosmith as early influences. While Jon's career has often been associated with Bruce Springsteen, he has been able to create his own identity through songwriting and forging his own unique career path. Springsteen's influence on the band has been discussed previously, and his legacy as a songwriter and presence in Asbury Park were greatly felt by Jon.

From his early days playing on the Jersey Shore, Jon has maintained a professional and personal relationship with Southside Johnny. His early exposure to the band greatly influenced his skills as a performer and musician. Similarly, his exposure to Southside Johnny increased his comfort level with the blues and their use in his songwriting. Jon mimics the vocals of Steven Tyler of Aerosmith a little on his first album but eventually finds his own unique voice. Bob Dylan's influence as a songwriter seems to hold personal significance for Jon. Richie Sambora gave Jon a gift of a guitar signed by Bob Dylan, which he regularly uses in performance. Phil Lynott of the Irish rock band Thin Lizzy was a dynamic front man like Jon, who composed or co-composed all the songs his band performed. Jon has cited this band as a major influence and obviously relates to Lynott, his staying power, and his prolific songwriting.

SONGWRITING

The success of the Rolling Stones, the Beatles, Aerosmith, U2, Led Zeppelin, and Bon Jovi is primarily due to the band members writing their own music. Jon and Richie Sambora have formed a classic songwriting brotherhood that seems prevalent in many rock bands, where lead singers and lead guitarists compose songs together: Mick Jagger and Keith Richards; John Lennon and Paul McCartney; Steve Tyler and Joe Perry; Bono and the Edge; and Jimmy Page and Robert Plant.

Bon Jovi and Sambora have spent more time with each other than with their own families; they traveled the world together and married their music careers and legacies to each other as songwriters. As a team they have written some of the most commercially successful rock songs of the past fifty years and built an impressive catalog of work. There was nothing especially extraordinary about the way they met. Richie Sambora described their first meeting:

> Alec [John Such] called me up and said, "hey man, you should come see, I'm playing with this Jon Bon Jovi band and you should come see us." And I said "cool." I just got into town, let me get back into circulation, and I went to see the band and I thought they were very good and I thought Johnny had a lot of charisma but I thought they were missing one thing . . . a guitar player.[1]

Richie played with the band during a rehearsal and impressed Jon. He was there to stay.

In the early days of Bon Jovi's career there seemed to be very little music that was stylistically situated between Metallica and Madonna. There was definitely an opening for the kind of music for which Bon Jovi would eventually become known: heavy American rock. Jon had some doubts about how his music would fit into the American musical scene. He reflected on those early days in a recent radio interview:

> I came from growing up listening to the J. Geils Band and listening to Southside Johnny and, you know, and it was an R and B regional successful kind of localized music if you will that had nothing to do with what was becoming very popular out of Los Angeles or the bands that we were opening for. . . . I had very little in common with any of 'em.[2]

Whatever trepidation Jon had about where his music fit into the lexicon was offset by his sheer ambition and determination to write successful songs. Jon and Richie were willing to do the hard work. Together they were able to create something out of nothing. Was the result largely influenced by other musicians? Yes. Did the music also have original elements? Yes.

In origin, Bon Jovi songs seem to spring from simple life experiences. Bon Jovi songs are grounded, not esoteric. Unlike U2, their songs do not take on a specific political issue. Unlike Metallica, their songs are not so angry that it is hard to discern a clear message. Unlike Aerosmith, their songs are more subtle in regard to sexuality. Bon Jovi and Sambora's writing has always started with an emotional perspective on a situation that they have experienced or deeply understand. For example, "Wanted Dead or Alive" is a song about their experience touring, and "Raise Your Hands" is a song about getting a concert crowd riled up and excited. The brilliance of the songs that convey these "simple" experiences is that listeners can relate their own feelings to the lyrics. Who hasn't had a boyfriend or girlfriend who turned out to be "Bad Medicine"? Everyone needs to sometimes hear the encouraging words "Keep the Faith." Who isn't "Livin' on a Prayer" that he makes it through? Relatable themes make good songs.

Jon and Richie's writing process is surprisingly informal. They get together with guitars, maybe a piano, and a tape recorder and come up with ideas. Several of their best songs were written at home in New Jersey. Jon remembers writing "Wanted Dead or Alive":

> The day that we sat down to write it we were home, we were in the basement of Richie's mother's house in Woodbridge, New Jersey. I woke Rich up . . . about one in the afternoon, when the sun was warm we'd get together and sit in that basement and knock one out before dinner and that was one of those good days when we wrote that and another one and it was done, start to finish, in an afternoon because God knows that the emotion was there for it.[3]

Jon Bon Jovi has described his songwriting process as starting with a song title, creating a chord structure, and finally writing the lyrics. Often musicians will begin with a lyric before creating the music.

Their grassroots approach has served them well as songwriters and businessmen. Jon has said that he considers himself a prolific writer and that there are plenty of songs to choose from when compiling a Bon Jovi album. In fact, they had so much unused material in 2004 that they put it all on a compilation album titled *100,000,000 Bon Jovi Fans Can't Be Wrong* and marketed it as the songs fans had never heard. The box set contains fifty songs, most of which had never been released. In the collaborative spirit of the band it includes songs composed by David Bryan. Drummer Tico Torres offers a rare vocal on one of the tracks.

Jon and Richie's longtime personal and professional relationship has maintained a collaborative spirit against all odds. Their level of success would seem to indicate that they share a creative vision when it comes to creating music. Apart from their solo projects, they have always maintained that they each take an equal part in writing and agree what direction the band wants to take artistically. Jon speaks often about the band's "vision." Richie seems to understand his relationship with the fans from the perspective of a songwriter:

> We're part of the fabric of people's lives at this point . . . as songwriters, but also as a band, we can stand up there and sing songs that people remember listening to the first time they made out in the car with somebody. It's a big privilege for us. When we walk out there and sing those songs, you see what's in the eyes of those people. We're singing about everybody.[4]

Despite the commercial songwriting success of the band, critics are quick to dismiss earned dollars as a sign of success. Jon Pareles of the *New York Times*: "Seasoned rock listeners are dismayed by the multi-million-record sales of a band that blatantly borrows from other rock while dispensing cliché upon cliché; hearing Bon Jovi is like being locked in a greeting-card warehouse with a radio that plays only 1970s classic rock."[5] This comment is indicative of the war that the critics would wage on Bon Jovi for the next twenty years.

One of the major reasons Bon Jovi is still relevant to today's music industry is that Jon and Richie Sambora can write good tunes. They are also able to write lyrics that are universally relatable. Good melodies and good lyrics equal good songs. Depending on one's perspective, Bon Jovi lyrics can be either banal or brilliant. The situations and stories of the songs are open-ended. They are common enough that people can transfer their own memories and emotions into the lyric and deeply, personally identify with the song. Perhaps this is a key reason that fans have made such a strong commitment to this band and have remained loyal. Fans are emotionally invested in the lyrics and music.

Of course this is true with much of popular music. Fans closely relating to a lyric is nothing new, but Bon Jovi has taken it to the next level. They seem to have the ability to tap into what their fans want to hear next and then deliver it. When peeled back to their core, the songs have themes that are as old as time. Faith, prayer, perseverance, love, and authenticity are just a few common themes in the lyrics. When delivered in a shiny and professional package, these messages are hard to resist.

Perhaps the common-man theme is not always intentional. Jon comments on his breakthrough single: "With 'It's My Life' I've written my most selfish song ever. At least that's what I thought. Until people picked up on the song, and applied it to themselves. They clearly thought it was THEIR life too."[6] People did think it was their life, and embraced it completely. "It's now or never, I ain't gonna live forever" is a mantra to which everyone can relate. Whether or not the lyric connection is always intentional, it is present between Bon Jovi and their audience.

Bon Jovi has connected with female fans from the first moment they stepped on a stage. The lyrics of Bon Jovi songs have not shied away from romantic themes. Lyrics like "I'll be there for you" and "I was born to be your man" and "diamond ring, wear it on your hand" have connected with female fans in an authentic way. Ballads like "I'll Be There for You," "Bed of Roses," "Always," and "Let's Make a Memory" are especially created to please women: romantic lyrics delivered by the rock god that is Jon Bon Jovi.

There have been some interesting stories in the press about how people relate to Bon Jovi songs. There was one story about a man who was absolutely convinced that listening to Bon Jovi songs lifted him out of a deep depression. Glenn Osrin had lost the job he loved and was spending most of every day in bed. He had lost his medical benefits and had trouble getting the help he needed. He has said: "This is where the music of Bon Jovi entered my life and helped me reprogram, rethink, and recharge my soul, saving my life in the process. That's right, Bon Jovi—the Man and the Band—saved my life . . . I was astounded to hear the relentlessly positive message throughout the entire album catalog."[7] Osrin goes on to explain how his wife, the right doctor, and medication, along with Bon Jovi, helped him regain his mental health. This type of reaction to the band's music does not seem to be unusual among fans. Osrin's reaction may be a real response to positive lyrics. At a 2010 Bon Jovi concert, a fifty-something man told the author a story about how his brother had recently died, and the only way he made it through was listening to Bon Jovi songs. He said he owed his sanity to the band.[8] Clearly, there is a substantive value for people in the message of Bon Jovi songs. The band has been publicly ridiculed for their choice of lyrics, that they are too simplified, romanticized, and unrealistic, but fans disagree. Bon Jovi has purposefully crafted a body of work that has an overall positive message. The fans have accepted the message and survived on it.

Audiences have continued to connect with Bon Jovi over a thirty-year career. The band's longevity has astounded music critics and the music industry as a whole. Perhaps the band's longevity is due to the fact that as they have aged, their music has matured and evolved. There is a notable difference between their earlier albums and 1992's *Keep the Faith* and later. Songs about current social issues and adult struggles began to replace songs about partying and chasing women. When pressed about why Bon Jovi's music is still around, Jon Bon Jovi has said that "it's music for the folks . . . it's folk music."[9] If the basic definition of folk music is music that is enjoyed by everyday people living their everyday lives, then Bon Jovi fits the bill. The critics may not agree, but relatable lyrics and good songwriting have worked for this band.

CAREER HIGHLIGHTS

There are a few musical moments in Bon Jovi's career that have had a real influence on the American culture at large. These moments are the *Slippery When Wet* album, the 2002 single "It's My Life" from the *Crush* album, the duet "Who Says You Can't Go Home" from the *Have a Nice Day* album, and the *Lost Highway* album.

Slippery When Wet (released in 1986) is undoubtedly considered Bon Jovi's breakthrough album. It was the best-selling album of 1987. It is also the most successful songwriting collaboration between Jon Bon Jovi and Richie Sambora. The singles "Livin' on a Prayer," "Wanted Dead or Alive," and "You Give Love a Bad Name" are still considered the gold standard of Bon Jovi singles. When *Slippery* came on the charts in 1986 it took the music industry by surprise. The album would eventually sell twenty-eight million copies worldwide, spend eight weeks at number one on the Billboard 200 chart, be certified "Diamond" by the Recording Industry Association of America, and become the twenty-first best-selling studio album of all time. In addition, with this album Bon Jovi became the first hard rock band to ever have two consecutive number one hits on the Billboard Hot 100 chart. One of the most astonishing aspects of the album was that no one expected a Bon Jovi album to do so incredibly well. It was literally a sensation. The combination of good timing, hit songs, and the first well-produced Bon Jovi music videos catapulted the album to legendary status in a remarkably short amount of time.

The album resulted in a worldwide tour that took Bon Jovi to North America, Japan, and Europe. The band was deluged with pandemonium everywhere they went. Huge crowds, screaming fans, and major media attention defined the Slippery When Wet Tour. Images of this excitement have been captured forever in the band's "Wanted Dead or Alive" video. In the video, we see the guys being protected from crazy fans grabbing for their clothes, the band being sped away from a massive arena show in shiny cars, and Jon staring out the window of a tour airplane contemplating the price of fame. Viewers got an inside glimpse of the dizzying world that is the rock world.

As songwriters, Bon Jovi and Sambora had a secret weapon on the *Slippery* album: Desmond Child. Songwriting wizard Child was brought into the writing process and shares credit for writing Bon Jovi's biggest hit, "Livin' on a Prayer." Child is known for collaborating with many different artists and has cowritten Aerosmith's "Crazy," "Angel," and "Dude (Looks Like a Lady)"; Ricky Martin's "Livin' la Vida Loca" and "She Bangs"; Ratt's "Shame Shame Shame"; and hits for more current performers like Katy Perry, Sisqó, Kelly Clarkson, and LeAnn Rimes. Child is a proven professional who can work with many different types of personalities. His musical signature is definitely written across a cross-section of popular American music. Bon Jovi has greatly benefitted from their association with Desmond Child; however, they do not necessarily openly give him credit for his contributions. From *Rolling Stone:* "Both Paul Stanley and Jon Bon Jovi refuse to discuss Child." Indeed, Bon Jovi, who said through a publicist that he was "very not interested in talking about Desmond," has eagerly reaped the commercial and artistic rewards of their collaboration.

Bon Jovi tells interviewers how proud he is to have written "Livin' on a Prayer"; he just doesn't mention that Child almost certainly played a bigger role in its creation. The only people who know who wrote "Livin' on a Prayer" are the three people who were in the room: Jon Bon Jovi, Richie Sambora, and Desmond Child. Richie Sambora remembers the day they wrote it: "So, anyway, I got there very late . . . I said, 'look, I got one word . . . prayer, and these chord changes.' It just kind of started there and then we all jumped in. At the end of the day we had the first verse and B section and the chorus . . . man, Jon and I got in the cab . . . and I go 'you know Jon this is gonna be a big song.'"[10] It is revealing that Desmond Child reused some of his own melodic material in work he did with Bon Jovi. Desmond Child's band Rouge produced a song titled "Our Love Is Insane" that is similar to "Livin' on a Prayer," and his composition for Bonnie Tyler titled "If You Were a Woman (And I Was a Man)" echoes "You Give Love a Bad Name." Of course, it is perfectly acceptable to borrow from yourself if you are a songwriter. With or without a writing partner, guitarist Richie Sambora agrees that *Slippery* is when it all came together for the songwriters: "Jon and I had a writing chemistry . . . but I don't think we really wrote any great songs until *Slippery*, and that was really when it came through."[11]

Another highlight of the band's career was the release of "It's My Life" from the *Crush* album in 2002. This song, from Bon Jovi's seventh studio album, was their most popular single in a decade. The band credits "It's My Life" for catching the attention of a whole new demographic of fans, who started listening to their music for the first time. In fact, there are millions of Bon Jovi fans who identify this album as their first Bon Jovi listening experience.

Bon Jovi comes full circle on this single by referencing Tommy and Gina, characters first introduced in "Livin' on a Prayer." It turns out they are doing great, they "never backed down." The continuation of Tommy and Gina's story is like an inside joke for Bon Jovi fans, more like a secret handshake. You need to know the 20th-century Bon Jovi to fully appreciate the 21st-century Bon Jovi.

"It's My Life" weaved its way into the fabric of American culture through massive exposure. Bon Jovi performed it at the groundbreaking Concert for New York City in 2001 at Madison Square Garden. The concert was a benefit concert and tribute to the men and women who served as police and fire personnel during the 9/11 crisis. In 2002, the song was featured in the closing ceremony of the Winter Olympic Games in Salt Lake City, Utah. Bon Jovi performed a small set that included "It's My Life." It would have been difficult to not have heard "It's My Life" in 2001 or 2002. The song resonated with the public as a new start for Bon Jovi.

"Who Says You Can't Go Home" was a critically important single for Bon Jovi. Recorded as a Bon Jovi song and later as a duet with Sugarland's Jennifer Nettles on 2005's *Have a Nice Day* album, the song represented several milestones in Bon Jovi's career. It peaked at number one on the country Billboard chart in 2005–2006 (a first for a rock band), and it won a Country Music Television (CMT) Award for Best Collaborative Video. In 2007, Bon Jovi won their first Grammy Award for Best Country Collaboration with Vocals (shared with Jennifer Nettles). Considering how quickly artists today seem to win Grammys, 1983 until 2007 seems like a long time for Bon Jovi to go without winning one.

In addition to several high-profile performances, "Who Says You Can't Go Home" was used as the centerpiece for a New Jersey state tourism council television campaign. It seems that New Jersey was finally proud of someone besides Bruce Springsteen.

The single's video was used as a conduit for the good works of Habitat for Humanity and featured Habitat volunteers building housing for low-income families alongside members of Jon Bon Jovi's Philadelphia Soul Arena Football League team. Bon Jovi got as much mileage out of this single as possible.

The most recent highlight of Bon Jovi's career is the album *Lost Highway*. Jon Bon Jovi described the album as a "Nashville-influenced Bon Jovi record,"[12] and despite this description, critics have endlessly compared it to a country record. It is not a country record, but an homage to the genre. Recording at Black Bird Studios in Nashville, Bon Jovi expanded their usual rock instrumentation to include the fiddle, harmonica, and mandolin, which gave the music a legitimate country sound. The album reached number one on the Billboard chart in July of 2007.

Bon Jovi's decision to do a Nashville project was no doubt a shrewdly calculated business move. The success of the Jennifer Nettles duet and the resulting Grammy proved that country music fans were willing to listen to Jon sing. It was a smart gamble. The success of the album guaranteed an entirely new demographic of fans. The Bon Jovi subgenre of country rock was perfectly timed. When the album came out, country music was more mainstream than it had ever been. Garth Brooks had paved the way for a more pop-friendly type of country music. The public was ready and willing to listen to something a little different, and Bon Jovi's original fan base was able to enjoy the album because it was not too country and was faithful to the familiar Bon Jovi sound. Over their career Bon Jovi has been building a relationship with Nashville and its musicians. They have performed and recorded there frequently. Jon became first on the country charts in 1998 when he recorded a duet with Chris LeDoux titled "Bang a Drum." Country artist Chris Cagle recorded a cover of Bon Jovi's "Wanted Dead or Alive." Jon Bon Jovi had worked with recording artist Keith Urban on the "Who Says You Can't Go Home" duet before deciding the duet would work better with a female partner. Bon Jovi had a comfortable familiarity with the country music community prior to the *Lost Highway* project. The band had made their mark in Nashville. However it all came together, *Lost Highway* was Bon Jovi's first number one album since 1988, and one of their four number one albums overall (*Slippery When Wet, New Jersey, Lost Highway, The Circle*). The Lost Highway Tour was the top-grossing tour of 2008, with $210.6 million in ticket sales.

The band's most recent album, *What About Now?*, was coproduced with veteran music producer John Shanks and released in 2013.

INDIVIDUAL SONGWRITING

The members of Bon Jovi work very well together as a band, but they also cherish working as solo artists. After recording and touring an album, the band will take a hiatus to rest, regroup, and create music apart from Bon Jovi. Jon, Richie Sambora, and David Bryan are all accomplished songwriters and have enjoyed solo careers. The musical experiences they have had in the band have influenced their solo writing as they have explored new genres and venues for composition. They have taken their vision of music to different audiences and, as a result, have created a much larger footprint in popular culture than they would have as only Bon Jovi.

Jon became involved with the film project *Young Guns II* (1990) after meeting Emilio Estevez through Ally Sheedy. The Hollywood lore is that the actor Emilio Estevez first approached Jon Bon Jovi about using his song "Dead or Alive" from the *Slippery* album. Jon suggested he would write something new for the film and came up with "Blaze of Glory." The rest went from there. He wrote a collection of songs for the film. The title track and the album were titled "Blaze of Glory" and were Bon Jovi's solo debut. This was not an ordinary side project. Some of the most popular actors of the day were in this movie: Emilio Estevez, Kiefer Sutherland, Christian Slater, and Lou Diamond Phillips. The film was a follow-up to the original *Young Guns* and grossed $44 million in the United States. The first songs that Jon Bon Jovi published on his own went on to gain much attention and many accolades. "Blaze of Glory" won a Golden Globe Award in 1991 and was nominated for an Oscar that same year. Bon Jovi's exposure from the *Young Guns II* experience drew more attention to Bon Jovi and highlighted the fact that Jon did not view himself as limited as to what he could accomplish.

He was noticed by the music and film industries. He even performed a tiny cameo in the film.

Jon has always embraced the cowboy culture, and he has brought that milieu to his fans and the greater public. Members of Bon Jovi have always enjoyed featuring cowboy couture. Richie Sambora loves weaering a cowboy hat during an arena rock show, and cowboy boots have been featured on several albums. Jon has a large tattoo of a steer with horns on his right arm. His film experience with *Young Guns II* indulged this interest further, with a video shoot for "Blaze of Glory" in the red desert with Jon on top of a huge rock wearing a Native American/rock star hybrid outfit. Bon Jovi's hugely popular single "Wanted Dead or Alive" evokes the Wild West as Jon sings: "I'm a cowboy; on a steel horse I ride." The cowboy theme makes an appearance in two songs on the *New Jersey* album: "Ride Cowboy Ride" and "Stick to Your Guns." A single that did not make the *Lost Highway* album titled "Put the Boy Back in Cowboy" was hugely popular on the Internet. Jon and Dorothea Bon Jovi named their son Jesse James. The band's association with Nashville and the *Lost Highway* project supported the cowboy image as well. In a 2004 *Billboard* interview, Jon gave an unusually personal insight into his idea of the cowboy:

> Another dawn on a highway, there was a romantic version of that. There was the feeling that you, in clichéd terms, rode into town, took the money, met the girls, drank their booze, and left before they caught you and that was the cute way I would describe it as a 25-year-old. As I got older . . . it was more the life of a traveling salesman. But the romantic version in my 20s was that of a cowboy.[13]

The analogy makes sense, but it is surprising that Jon Bon Jovi would admit to that lifestyle.

Destination Anywhere was Jon Bon Jovi's second solo album and was released in 1997. The album had a companion short film, which was released the same year. The film features Demi Moore, Kevin Bacon, Whoopi Goldberg, and Annabella Sciorra, along with Jon Bon Jovi. David Bryan and Desmond Child contributed to the album. *Destination Anywhere* was not a big commercial success and received lukewarm reviews.

Richie Sambora was an accomplished professional guitarist and sang lead vocals in bands prior to Bon Jovi. It makes sense that he would release two solo albums. Through solo work, he is able to feature himself as a singer as well as a guitarist and songwriter. *Stranger in This Town*, released in 1991, is Sambora's debut solo album. Bon Jovi members David Bryan and Tico Torres play on this album, and guest guitarist Eric Clapton plays on one track. The tunes are blues-influenced, and several are cowritten by David Bryan. Richie Sambora wrote or cowrote all the songs. Despite Sambora's efforts, the reviews were less than glowing. An example from *Entertainment Weekly's* David Browne: "most of the album resembles the blowsy pop-metal of Whitesnake on a really bad day."[14] Even as a solo artist, Sambora cannot escape the reference to the "hair band" genre. Bon Jovi was working very hard to disassociate itself from the hair band genre. A reference to Whitesnake in a review of Sambora's album would have been tough to take. His second solo album, *Undiscovered Soul*, was released in 1998. Again, Sambora wrote or cowrote all the tunes, most with Richie Supa. David Bryan contributed to the writing again as well. Reviews for this album were mixed.

David Bryan is not thought of as a songwriter in the context of Bon Jovi, although he did receive writing credit for the Bon Jovi hit "In These Arms." Because of his diverse writing interests, he may turn out to be the most accomplished writer of anyone in the band. He has composed for several genres, including song, piano, film soundtracks, and musical theater. He has also composed songs for other artists, like Curtis Stigers. He composed music for the film *Netherworld*, released in 1992. Bryan has writing credits on the Bon Jovi albums *Bon Jovi* and *Keep the Faith*, as well as others. He contributed as a writer to Richie Sambora's two solo albums in addition to releasing two solo albums of his own. *On a Full Moon*, released in 1995, is David Bryan's debut instrumental solo album. *Lunar Eclipse*, 2000, is his follow-up solo album. It is a compilation of pieces for solo piano. Bryan says, "Piano playing is a dying art. I love the fact that I can be one guy with one instrument evoking an emotional and musical experience."[15]

THE PMRC EFFECT

In the mid-1980s, politics and the music business collided in an unexpected way. Censorship was alive and well in America. For the first time in music industry history, active steps were taken to "protect" children from the harmful effects of rock and heavy metal music and lyrics. Actions taken by the Parents Music Resource Center (PMRC) would have a major influence on American songwriters and musicians and the culture at large.

The PMRC was created by a group of political Washington, D.C., wives and was supposedly nonpartisan. The future vice-presidential spouse Mrs. Tipper Gore, Susan Baker, Pam Howard, and Sally Nevius were the core group of women to formally establish the PMRC. They claimed their mission was to increase parental control over children's access to music that was considered especially "violent." Suggestions by the PMRC included printed warnings on albums for sale, altered covers on certain recordings, and the eventual censorship of various videos and songs. As a result of their actions, certain music was banned, and removed from stores like Wal-Mart, Sears, and J.C. Penney.

The PMRC's main legacy was the creation of the "Filthy Fifteen," a list of fifteen songs and artists that the Center found most offensive. Interestingly enough, only two of the fifteen songs have references to violence in their lyrics. Most of the songs reference sexual activity of some kind or drug and alcohol use. A few of the songs are labeled as being related to the occult. Tipper Gore spoke about the fact that her daughter had brought Prince's song "Darling Nikki" to her attention, and this is when she realized she had to do something to protect the children. Ironically, "Darling Nikki" is about sex, not violence, and does not support the mission statement of the Center. Other persecuted artists on the list included Cyndi Lauper, Judas Priest, Mötley Crüe, AC/DC, Twisted Sister, Def Leppard, Black Sabbath, and Madonna.

Long before "family values" became the nation's catch phrase for all morality, the PMRC was preaching about moral responsibility to our children. In September of 1985, a formal hearing began in front of the U.S. Senate Committee on Commerce, Science, and Transportation. Musicians Frank Zappa, John Denver, and Dee Snider of Twisted Sister appeared before the Senate as opposing witnesses and spoke plainly against censorship.

At some point during the testimony, the Recording Industry Association of America (RIAA) agreed to put "Parental Advisory" stickers on some releases of their choosing. This was the only mandated outcome from the hearing, but the whole process sent waves of disdain through the music industry and general public. There was fallout from the hearing and the decision by the RIAA. Many different artists expressed their ire through music and in the press. Heavy metal artists were primarily targeted on the Filthy Fifteen lists, and the music community hit back the best way they could—through music. The following bands are just a sampling of musicians who responded to the PMRC with lyrics in their songs, in videos, and by placing faux labels on their album covers: Megadeth, Metallica, Ice-T, Quiet Riot, Sonic Youth, Cinderella, Warrant, Guns N' Roses, and Aerosmith.

Besides being a part of the community of artists affected by the PMRC, Bon Jovi was also impacted in another way. When selecting the album cover for what would become their biggest album, *Slippery When Wet*, the influence of Tipper Gore and the PMRC kept them from using their original choice. The woman wearing a wet yellow T-shirt that read "Slippery When Wet" was replaced with the black trash bag cover known today. It is difficult to know whether the move was a preemptive strike or a response to a dictate from the record company, but the censorship culture of the day had a direct influence. In a 1987 *Creem* interview, Jon had some plain thoughts about the PMRC situation: "We have a song on this album called 'Social Disease' that has a lot to do with certain establishments. It's a tribute to penicillin. We're dedicating it to Tipper Gore. She's so off the mark that she'll just jump right down its throat and not even read the lyrics to see what it's about. I'm going to take her daughter out, just to piss her off."[16] It is possible that Bon Jovi's strong feelings about Gore and the PMRC were the impetus for his involvement in politics. Ironically, Jon would go on to support Al and Tipper Gore politically in their vice-presidential and presidential races.

RECOGNITION AS SONGWRITERS

In the third decade of their career as Bon Jovi, Jon Bon Jovi and Richie Sambora are finally starting to receive some recognition for their contributions to American rock music after being discounted by the music critics. In 2009, they were inducted into the Songwriters Hall of Fame. The organization was founded in 1969 by songwriter Johnny Mercer and publishers Howie Richmond and Abe Olman. Jon and Richie's induction puts them on an exclusive list of inductees, who include Jerry Leiber and Mike Stoller, Bob Dylan, Bruce Springsteen, Dolly Parton, Leonard Cohen, James Brown, Elton John, and Billy Joel. At the 2009 induction, singer Chris Daughtry honored the songwriters by performing one of their hit songs, "I'll Be There for You." Daughtry had toured with Bon Jovi as an opening act in the past. At the same ceremony, Jon and Richie performed their iconic "Wanted Dead or Alive."

Two years later, in 2011, Bon Jovi was announced as a nominee for the Rock and Roll Hall of Fame. Nominees were required to have released an album prior to 1985 to be nominated in 2011. Other nominees that year included Alice Cooper, the Beastie Boys, Neil Diamond, LL Cool J, and Tom Waits. Bon Jovi was not selected as an inductee. This was the first nomination for Bon Jovi.

As a band, Bon Jovi holds two very special records. Their 1986 album, *Slippery When Wet*, made Bon Jovi the first hard rock band to have two consecutive number one Billboard Hot 100 chart hits. They are also the first band to have a number one hit on the rock and country charts at the same time: "Who Says You Can't Go Home." Their commercial success, wealth, and loyal fans have sustained them despite a continuing harsh reception from critics. What the future holds for the band is uncertain; however, disparagement from critics has historically driven the band to new creative heights.

3

MTV'S BAND FOR A GENERATION

"I WANT MY MTV"!

MTV (Music TeleVision) was the brainchild of music executives who thought it would be a good idea to play music videos on television twenty-four hours a day, seven days a week. The first video aired on August 1, 1981 (the Buggles' "Video Killed the Radio Star") and changed the face of music forever. MTV featured mainstream rock songs and albums. Racial and musical diversity did not come until later (Michael Jackson's first video, "Billie Jean," was one of the first diverse videos on MTV). Programming was hosted by "VJs" or "veejays" (video jockeys), who ranged in age and type: there were a boy and girl next door, a hard rocker, the brainy girl, etc. The executives at MTV arranged it so they would not pay for videos; the record labels were responsible for funding their artists' videos. By playing videos constantly, the channel and record companies were able to promote and sell records while they were asleep in their beds. The videos sold records. MTV was a hugely lucrative endeavor, which eventually became completely commercially driven and turned into a reality channel. But in the beginning, it was totally new, inventive, and special.

Today's youth may find it hard to conceive of this, but MTV was the one thing the kids of the '80s did together besides go to school. There was no Facebook or social networking, nor was there a vast selection of cable networks. MTV was something kids watched at home, sometimes with friends, and it was a truly collective experience. One could live in

New York City, Tampa, Santa Fe, or Petaluma and be watching the exact same video at the exact same time. Videos that had recently debuted on MTV were discussed at school the next day. MTV was a singular development in popular culture.

Besides playing music videos, MTV produced unique programs that defined a generation. *Remote Control* was the original non-music program on MTV. Set up in a game-show format, it featured comedians like Denis Leary, Colin Quinn, and Adam Sandler in their early careers. The network facilitated hip-hop's transition to the mainstream worldwide with *Yo! MTV Raps*. *Rockumentary* and *TRL* were other examples of innovative programming. Shows from more recent years include *The Osbournes, The Hills*, and *Beavis and Butt-Head*. Perhaps one of the most memorable examples of non-music programming on MTV was the Rock the Vote campaign. In 1992, MTV paired with famous artists of the day to encourage young people to get involved in the political process, and more specifically to get out and vote in the presidential election. Public service announcements were broadcast; as a result, the youth voters increased twenty percent from the previous presidential election, and the movement facilitated the registration of 350,000 new young voters.[1] Candidate Bill Clinton participated in a Rock the Vote town hall meeting, where he was famously asked, "boxers or briefs?" (Answer: briefs.) His willingness to answer the question spoke for itself. His opponent, President George Bush, refused to go on MTV.

The success of the original reality show *The Real World* ensured the decline of music video programming on MTV. With that show, MTV started to become a different kind of network. Kids began to tune in to MTV to watch a reality soap opera, not music videos. The arrival of reality programming had long-reaching effects on the music industry, musical artists, and television in general. Retrospection spurs truth: "Of all MTV's long-form programming, *The Real World* had the most tenuous connection to music. Its success speeded video's dismissal from TV and was bad news for record labels: MTV had thought to make themselves independent of the labels, but the labels never thought to make themselves independent of MTV."[2] A complete shift in programming and the place of the music video on MTV resulted in the removal of the words "music television" from its logo in 2010.

One of the biggest effects of MTV was the new cultural norm of making music a visual experience. The way a singer looked suddenly became very, very important. Unlike Jon Bon Jovi, not everyone was comfortable with the reality. Former Capitol Records executive Mick Kleber reminisces: "Bonnie Raitt was one of the artists from the '70s who was nervous about making music videos. Bob Seger wasn't a huge fan of the idea of a music video. They were self-conscious about the still photos. You can imagine how uncomfortable they were with a video."[3] It seemed as if how an artist's looks were perceived could make or break them as a musical act. The music was now about visual, rather than aural, perception. Bon Jovi manager Doc McGhee makes an astute point about marketing the band: "The concept is simple: show people what you want them to believe you are. So I showed them crazy rock bands, with chicks everywhere, and people staring up at the stage in awe."[4] (In the music business, women are often referred to as "chicks.")

The result of this new visual reality was that a band had to have their style and image completely ingrained before their first video aired on MTV. There was no room or time for mistakes. Mark Mothersbaugh, cofounder of Devo: "Bands had to go for gold right away. MTV got all the money you were making. So you were paying for MTV's programming, instead of surviving for a year as a band. It's no accident the term 'one-hit wonder' is centered around the '80s. MTV destroyed the idea of a band being able to do an album or two before they made their *magnum opus*, or before they made their strong statement. Videos changed the economics of the industry."[5]

The role of women in rock and roll seems to have always been controversial. The music video took that to new heights when it came to male bands. Former CEO of MTV Networks Judy McGrath comments: "The hair metal bands loved MTV and they had a huge number of fans. But their videos promoted the objectification of women. There were years here when it was hard to be a woman."[6] MTV made it possible for young women to see bands they would probably never see live on the TV in their living rooms. It brought women a comfort level with rock bands that they had not had previously. It was much easier to get excited about going to a Bon Jovi concert after seeing one of their entertaining videos on MTV over and over. From the beginning, Jon Bon Jovi's appeal was evident when it came to women: "Ever since the '70s, loud rock has traditionally been the preserve of a predominantly male audience. Then MTV helped bring Bon Jovi to millions of young women as well. In the video for the group's greatest hit, 'Wanted Dead or Alive,' from the 1986 album *Slippery When Wet,* Bon Jovi's attraction was that he looked positively vulnerable."[7]

The death of the music video and MTV as the supreme delivery device of it came quickly as the Internet developed as an everyday tool. Any music video could be viewed at any time on a computer screen, at home or anywhere else. The general public did not need MTV anymore. The Golden Age of music videos had come to an end: "Most of the people who created the video industry agree that by '92, the Golden Age was winding down. Videos were now carefully controlled by record labels, minimizing the chance of imaginative work."[8]

MTV AS *THE* MARKETING TOOL

Whether the executives at MTV intended for their channel to be a commercial for rock albums or an artistic medium to enlighten and inspire, we'll never know. There were artistic and creative music videos made all the time. The simple fact was that a successful video, requested often and put in heavy rotation, sold albums; it made money. The channel could not help but be a commercial medium in which artists wanted to succeed.

One of the bands to benefit the most from MTV was Bon Jovi. There is no question that their most successful videos ("Wanted Dead or Alive" and "Livin' on a Prayer") had a very positive effect on their image. The majority of their fans today first came to know the band through the images projected in those videos, and they still go to see them in concert. MTV was Bon Jovi's ultimate marketing tool in the 1980s, and they understood and thrived in the medium after a rocky start.

The original concept of MTV was to feature "album rock." The heavy metal genre was a natural offshoot of that, and many of those bands did very well at MTV. Van Halen is one example of a band that was favored by the MTV network, and their videos were played in heavy rotation. Heavy metal and pop ruled the network for a long time, but the grunge genre changed everything. The arrival of bands like Nirvana and Pearl Jam changed the landscape of the music video. Nirvana's record-breaking single, "Smells Like Teen Spirit," was turned into a video that astounded the music industry and enraptured viewers with its fresh approach to the then-current concept of the music video.

Before the arrival of grunge, when heavy metal dominated video airplay, Bon Jovi's manager, Doc McGhee, was carefully manipulating the band's image: "Jon said, 'Why can't we have our own guy?' And I go, 'Because you've done bad videos. Sorry, we're not standing on the boardwalk like the Beatles. We're a f—— rock band.' I wanted their videos to be like Mötley Crüe, but fun. Let's see Johnny's million-dollar smile. That's what sold Johnny."[9]

Everyone in the band wanted to move forward after the bad experience with their first video, "Runaway." They found their savior in the video director Wayne Isham. The music video director had a direct influence on the marketing of a band. Guns N' Roses' former manager Alan Niven: "I'm not sure how well that band would have done before MTV. One track off their first album worked, 'Runaway.' Their second album was not good. Had it not been for Jon's good looks, I'm not sure Bon Jovi would have been allowed to make a third album. Wayne Isham was at least as important to that band as Jon Bon Jovi."[10]

Bon Jovi took their share of hits in regard to their videos from their metal colleagues and critics in the written press. MTV had a show called *Headbangers Ball* that played metal videos late at night. It seemed that, even at three AM, Bon Jovi could not catch a break. VJ Adam Curry recalls the time: "If I'm recognized in public now, it's always about *Headbangers Ball*. Sure, we had to play Bon Jovi videos. But Saturday at midnight, for three hours, we'd play Metallica, Anthrax, Iron Maiden. . . . I always got asked, "Hey man, why are you playing Bon Jovi? This is our three hours."[11]

Another example of the metal community not embracing Bon Jovi was Metallica. Lead singer James Hetfield was not a Bon Jovi fan. Former MTV executive Robin Sloane remembers: "At the 'One' video, James Hetfield had a sticker on his guitar that read, F— Bon Jovi." I said, 'You have to cover that up, or MTV will not play this.' . . . he refused to cover it. So I told the director, Bill Pope, to shoot in a way that no one can see the sticker."[12]

One of the most successful marketing schemes MTV employed was the contest. Band management and MTV executives would come up with a promotional contest for a band and give away a prize to the winning contestant from the public entries. Bon Jovi was certainly part of the contest blitz in the early days. The first contest they promoted was the giveaway of Jon's childhood home in Sayreville, New Jersey. In 1989, the Bongiovi family, Jon's parents and brothers, were moving from the house Jon had lived in during his younger years. MTV offered the house, valued at $200,000; a check for the property taxes; and a Kawasaki motorcycle to the winning contestant. Out of the one million people entered in the contest, young couple Judy and Jay Frappier were the winners. They were treated to a house tour by Jon Bon Jovi himself and were presented with the deed to the house, the check, and the motorcycle in front of the entire ogling neighborhood and many MTV cameras. As happy as the Frappiers were to win the house, it did not turn out to be the dream come true they had hoped. A year later, they sold the house and moved after receiving a $70,000 property tax bill.[13] The former Bongiovi family home has changed ownership several times since 1989, but is still an attractive house in a well-kept, lovely neighborhood in the thriving Parlin area of Sayreville. The contest was created to promote Bon Jovi's album *New Jersey*.

In 1987, MTV featured a contest called "Hedonism Weekend with Bon Jovi." The four winners spent a weekend in Negril, Jamaica, with VJs from MTV and the band. The edginess of the television coverage of the event was limited to drummer Tico Torres in a black Speedo, drinking Red Stripe. The band frolicked with Jamaican natives and the winners, playing games on the beach and introducing videos. It is most likely that the band did not have a stylist along with them. Jon featured a pair of faded blue-jean cutoff shorts and mirrored sunglasses: that's all. Richie Sambora was the most distinguished-looking of the group.

THE VIDEOS

It is surprisingly fascinating to take a look back at Bon Jovi's video discography over the past almost thirty years. When a band endures as long as Bon Jovi has, it only makes sense that their music and videos would change over time. The videos serve as a living yearbook of Bon Jovi's video hits and misses. What follows here is a brief retrospective of some of the band's most well-known videos.

"Runaway," Bon Jovi's very first video, was off the *Bon Jovi* album and was discussed in a previous chapter. Even though the band despised the video concept, they managed to hide that fact while filming and came across as professional. Jon showed much promise despite the fact that he was wearing lilac leather pants. Their own manager, Doc McGhee, did not have anything nice to say about the "Runaway" experience: "I'd just started to manage Bon Jovi when we did the video for 'Runaway.' There's a chubby girl who's a runaway, but she has laser eyes, and the band is playing in a warehouse that's burning." Jon Bon Jovi would go on to insult this poor girl again in *Creem* magazine, when he claimed that there "would never, ever, as long as I live, be another ugly girl in my videos . . . uhhh, don't say anything about the ugly girls, 'cause they probably read the magazine."[14] (The young beauty in the video is actually quite stunning and probably a size four.) "She Don't Know Me" was a single off the same album, but the song was written by Marc Avec, not Bon Jovi. The song had noticeably more '80s instrumentation than other songs on the record. It was not a revolutionary video, story-based and not at all fantastical like the first video off the album. A major difference from the first video is that the focus is on Jon Bon Jovi to the exclusion of the rest of the band. The other four guys make extremely brief appearances in between the verses when Jon is singing. It is clear that Jon was intended to be the focus of the video. It is possible to see the beginning of the actor in Jon coming out, as he has the opportunity to display some acting chops in this video, especially during the camera close-ups.

"She Don't Know Me" may be the video that inspired the classification of "hair band" in the '80s. Each of the guys' hair is teased to the sky, with the exception of Tico Torres (you get the feeling he would not let the stylist near his head). David Bryan suffers the most, as his coiffure reaches a good twelve inches above his head. Much preparation has gone into Jon's hairstyle as well, and blond highlights are perfectly and strategically placed.

By the second album, *7800° Fahrenheit* (1985), the executives, management, and band had caught on to the fact that their videos should feature more live performance; therefore, live performance scenes are spliced in between scenes of the guys having fun at the beach in the video "In and Out of Love." The video is more successful than any others up to this point in the sense that it has a basic story line and the personalities of the guys have a chance to come out; in addition, the entire band is featured, instead of only Jon. The background for the video is the charming Seaside Heights, New Jersey.

Bon Jovi's biggest album, *Slippery When Wet*, was released in 1986. The mega best seller produced a trifecta of music videos that solidified the band's image. The *Slippery* videos elevate Bon Jovi to legendary music video status. The other factor that makes these videos stand out is the band's involvement with director Wayne Isham. Their relationship with him made their videos a success. Isham has directed Bon Jovi videos throughout their career, from "You Give Love a Bad Name" to "It's My Life." In the '80s, he directed videos for musical acts like Whitney Houston and Howard Jones but excelled in the heavy metal genre with bands like Mötley Crüe, Def Leppard, Ozzy Osbourne, and Skid Row. The band's first collaboration with Wayne Isham was "You Give Love a Bad Name." The video finally finds a basic style for the band in the music video genre. Isham features a live performance of the song that exudes the raw energy that Bon Jovi produces onstage. It also capitalizes on the back-and-forth of the excited fans and the guys on-stage. Fashion-wise, it is high '80s rock and roll couture. Richie Sambora has shoulder pads, Tico Torres has a super-long mullet, and Alec John Such has on his Cuban boots; however, the biggest fashion victim is keyboardist David Bryan. He is wearing a jacket with sheer black sleeves so complicated even Stevie Nicks would refuse to wear it. Of course, at the time, the fans really liked what they were wearing, and most of it was not very different from other current bands of the day. The overall effect is a new Bon Jovi and a band that is finding a comfort level they can live with in the music video genre.

It turns out that Jon Bon Jovi's career wisdom grew with experience and age. Wayne Isham recalls that Jon Bon Jovi had his own concepts for the first video off the *Slippery* album: "Jon had his own ideas for 'You Give Love a Bad Name.' He wanted chicks in low-cut tops and mud wrestling. That wasn't what I was about. I know it sounds funny, coming from the guy who directed Mötley Crüe's 'Girls, Girls, Girls,' but there's a world of difference between the burlesque in 'Girls, Girls, Girls' and mud wrestling."[15] Isham created a totally new atmosphere for the video. Shot at the unused Grand Olympic Auditorium in Los Angeles, a mock arena was constructed. Fans, lights, and sets were brought in to create concert realism. The video was a big success, and within a few weeks of its release, Bon Jovi was no longer opening for .38 Special but headlining their own show.

"Livin' on a Prayer" was the second video released from the album. This video is a standout both in Bon Jovi's career and in music video history. It is noteworthy for its sophisticated use of black-and-white film. The video shows the band on a huge stage in an empty arena having a great time. All of a sudden, the arena is full of adoring fans, and there is a wash of color. The band is in ripped jeans, boots, and black leather jackets; later, the wardrobe changes to something more ornate for the live-performance portion of the video. The video reveals quite a bit of the individual personalities and is extremely fun to watch.

"Wanted Dead or Alive" is the third video released from the album. This video is entirely black and white and reveals a road-weary and exhausted Bon Jovi. You feel their pain while watching the video. Every cliché about being a rock star is included: demanding groupies, planes, trains, buses, and automobiles, alcohol, road crew, live performance, backstage, the dressing room. It's all there. Yet somehow, there is a truth to it, and it is believable. Bon Jovi is suffering for their art. While watching this video on MTV, teens were able to see themselves relating to the band as concertgoers. The previous three videos, especially "Dead or Alive," were influential on many videos that followed: "Through their partnership with Wayne, they produced some of the most influential performance-driven videos and also the 'band on the road' theme. 'Dead or Alive,' 'Livin' on a Prayer,' 'You Give Love a Bad Name'; those videos were absolutely huge and influential and, I think, copied for years."[16] Other artists of the day, even Metallica, appreciated the video. Lars Ulrich: "Maybe my favorite video of the '80s was 'Wanted Dead or Alive.' Wayne Isham brilliantly captured the other side of rock 'n' roll. . . . Wayne was by far the number one guy in rock videos."[17]

Bon Jovi's second blockbuster album, 1988's *New Jersey*, spawned several popular videos, including "Bad Medicine," "Born to Be My Baby," "Livin' in Sin," and "Blood on Blood." The "Bad Medicine" video is a steamy, sweaty romp in which audience members (mostly scantily clad young women) were given video cameras to film the band. The result is a jolting, chaotic series of quick shots. The band is still performing live in an arena, but it is not a cohesive or sophisticated concept for a video. It comes off as less artistic and more cheaply done than the highly successful *Slippery* videos.

"Born to Be My Baby" is a feel-good fun video in a way that "Bad Medicine" was not. Viewers get a close-up look at the band in the recording studio and a "behind the scenes" view of the process of re-cording a single. The choice of black and white is a good one, and director Wayne Isham manages to give the video an almost epic feel in a very small space. The guys give a shout-out to New Jersey with Jon wearing a "Shore Baseball" sweatshirt and Alec John Such wearing a New Jersey T-shirt. The video is special for its super-quick view of Dorothea Hurley receiving a hug from her soon-to-be husband, Jon.

"Livin' in Sin" is another video offering from *New Jersey*. The video features the story line of a young couple living together and disappoint-ing their parents and priest. The story of the video is spliced with shots of the band playing in a small studio space. The action of the story fits well with the tempo and mood of the song.

"Blood on Blood" is really the quintessential Bon Jovi song. It's a song about brotherhood, staying together through tough times, and remembering what is important. Listening to the lyrics, one believes that Danny and Bobby are real guys. It is tight musically, and the grainy black-and-white video puts the focus on the music rather than a rock spectacle. The video is a little bit of a turning point for the band. Alec John Such was the first band member to cut his hair short, and Jon is wearing the tightest black leather pants of his career, but there is a new maturity to the group and they have settled into a groove as a band.

When the album *Keep the Faith* was released in 1992, the band had been on hiatus for several years. The band looked at the *Keep the Faith* project as kind of a recommitment to their life as a band. The popular "Bed of Roses" is one of the videos off that record. Again in black and white, and featuring close-ups of Jon, the video lacks a concept. It is part story-based, part behind the scenes, part recording session, part live performance, and part on a huge pile of rocks somewhere in the Southwest. The overall effect is that of someone who could not make up his mind about what the video was going to be. Jon has famously cut his hair short by this time and is wearing a pair of hoop earrings.

"Keep the Faith" is another video off the record. Watching this video today, one cannot help but think there was a missed opportunity here. This is one of the band's more edgy songs, and the video just doesn't live up to the quality of the music. Ninety-five percent of the video is a close-up of Jon's face and hair (it is not permed and teased; it is hot-rolled and teased, then smoothed). In live performance, this is one of the band's best songs, and the video is a disappointment.

The album *These Days* was released in 1995. "Something for the Pain" is one video off the record and is an ill-conceived low point in the band's video history. It is loosely based on the story of a teenage boy having a virtual experience with Bon Jovi and friends. The most notable thing about the video is that Tico Torres has cut his hair. This is the first video without former band member Alec John Such.

"These Days" is the title video off the album, and it features the band on a world tour across Asia and Africa. It splices shots of the guys interacting with indigenous people with live performance. Like "Wanted Dead or Alive," the "These Days" video is of the on-the-road genre, but it is missing the heart of "Wanted."

In 2001, Bon Jovi used video director Wayne Isham again to good effect, in the video for their hit song "It's My Life" off the *Crush* album. In the video, everyone in the band looks sleeker and more polished than in the past. Isham shoots a performance scenario in a subway tunnel, and the audience is packed with very young fans. There is an artistic hue of blue, black, and silver over the entire scene. This is also a story-based video, with a young leading man trying to get to his girlfriend in the tunnel. It is easy to see that the video was constructed to attract a younger audience than the band's original fan base. It seems to work. The video has a young feel to it.

The video for "Everyday," from 2002's *Bounce* album, takes a shot at larger-than-life themes such as unity and music as a catalyst for uniting the world's people. The song "Everyday" may or may not have been a reaction to the events of September 11, 2001. Although the band made a brave choice in making reactionary music to the events of 9/11, the video is not a reflection of the event. There are interesting scenic views of the Very Large Array in Socorro, New Mexico.

The album *Have a Nice Day* was released in 2005, and the title video has a fresh feel to it. The star of the video is the twisted red smiley-face logo that appears all over Manhattan. Again, the video is filled with images of young fans enjoying Bon Jovi performing.

The partner video from this album is for the song "Who Says You Can't Go Home" (no question mark at the end of the sentence). This may be the best Bon Jovi video since the *Slippery* album. As always, the band comes across best when they are engaged in whatever they are doing in real life. The video is filmed in Philadelphia, as members of Habitat for Humanity are working on a project. The video is directed so the rest of the band's personalities, not just Jon's, come through. It is clear to see that all are having a good time.

"You Want to Make a Memory" from the 2007 album *Lost Highway* is a quiet video that features Jon Bon Jovi. It is significant in that it may be the first video in which Jon is wearing a wedding ring. "I Love This Town" is another single from the album. The video features a live Bon Jovi performance and shots of several different baseball teams goofing off, having fun, and playing baseball. There is kind of a feel that the town Bon Jovi is singing about is whatever town the listener lives in. It is a catchy concept that resonates with a male audience.

Bon Jovi's album *The Circle* was released in 2009. (*Greatest Hits* was released in 2010). The video for "We Weren't Born to Follow" was used to promote the album. Performing on a rooftop is not a new concept for a music video, but the images of Princess Diana, 9/11, Nelson Mandela, Bobby Kennedy, Barack Obama, and Martin Luther King Jr. are hard to fault.

The relevancy and importance of music videos have changed significantly since the beginning of Bon Jovi's career. With the evolution of the Internet and the dominance of reality television, the music video has become less crucial to a band's success than it was in the '80s. Today, many music acts publish their videos directly to YouTube or other Internet venues. Bon Jovi has continued to make videos as part of their marketing campaign for new albums, but it is a perfunctory gesture. The band is known for their live performance and not their videos.

MTV AWARDS

It only makes sense that MTV would eventually have an awards show. The MTV Video Music Awards honored music artists for their achievements in video and the music industry (later would come the MTV Movie Awards). It does not seem cutting-edge now, but in 1984 the production was *the* anti-establishment, anti-Grammy venue for all of the world's music stars to make their mark. The major difference between the MTV Video Music Awards and similar shows today is that in 1984 there was no "cable" television, and there were not nearly as many choices as to what to watch. It was a time when every family did not necessarily have a VCR in their home. People still checked the television listings at the beginning of the week to see what would be on Friday and Saturday nights.

For MTV, the awards were all about the commercial market and the pushing of their product: the musical artist. Kids thought they were getting a special inside look at their favorite musical groups. MTV executives were selling advertising like crazy. The idea to give awards to the acts on their own network? Brilliant.

The very first MTV Awards took place in New York City on September 14, 1984. Hosted by Bette Midler and Dan Aykroyd, the show served to reinforce the significance of the music video in America's youth culture. The inaugural show featured a legendary performance by Madonna of her hit "Like a Virgin." Compared with what is seen on MTV Awards shows today, Madonna's performance seems tame, but it was a major event that was discussed in the mainstream media. It is hard to forget her rolling around on the floor in a tacky white wedding dress, lace gloves, and a "Boy Toy" belt buckle. No one had ever seen anything like that before, and that was the whole point. Other networks, like VH1, would try to imitate the success of MTV with their own awards shows.

It is worth noting that the MTV Awards had to deal with the reality of the Parents Music Resource Center (PMRC) and general censorship at the 1990 awards. In fact, the repercussions of Tipper Gore's pet project were felt in the industry for years, and even today. As a network, MTV was very familiar with censorship in America. Artists pushed the envelope of what they could get away with from the beginning. They were not immune to the far-reaching effects of the PMRC and the wrath of Tipper Gore. MTV had its own system of review: "MTV had been asking bands to edit and tone down videos ever since 'Girls on Film.' By the time of the PMRC hearings, the network had created a formal system of review, in which a (one-person) standards and practices department examined every video before it could air. Officially, MTV had a policy against excessive sex or violence—though to the delight of most viewers, the policy proved to be pretty flexible."[18]

Some in the music industry believe that a Bon Jovi live performance at the MTV Awards was the beginning of the hugely successful *Unplugged* series on the network. Bon Jovi was not the first band to perform acoustically (a stripped-down, non-electronic musical performance) on MTV. On the Awards in 1989 they did perform one of the most well-known acoustic sets ever to air on television. There continues to be controversy as to whether or not Bon Jovi's performance influenced the hugely successful MTV show *Unplugged*. The popularity of Jon and Richie Sambora's set at the awards show made a big impression: "An upcoming episode featuring Bon Jovi—who some say inspired the program with their acoustic set at the 1989 MTV Video Music Awards—will be presented in three variations on different channels."[19]

MTV AS A CULTURAL INFLUENCE

There is no doubt that MTV and Bon Jovi on MTV both had an influence on American and world culture during the 1980s. The genre of "music video" highlighted dance and fashion in tandem with music in a way that had not previously been done. The visual medium influenced what kids were wearing; how an artist dressed greatly affected the way he and his music were perceived.

One of the reasons MTV was in a position to influence its teenage audience is that it was the first television programming focused on that audience. Teens were waiting and ready for the phenomenon: "The MTV aesthetic during its Golden Age of 1981–1992—quick cuts, celebrations of youth, shock value, impermanence, beauty—influenced not only music, but network and cable TV, radio, advertising, film, art, fashion, race, teen sexuality, even politics. The channel was plotted to captivate an audience whose interests had been ignored: John Lack, who started MTV, called teenagers 'the demographic group least interested in TV,' because TV wasn't interested in teens. . . . MTV gave them what they wanted, and got them not only interested in, but obsessed by MTV, making it their clubhouse."[20] The channel's catchphrase "I Want My MTV" really did reflect how viewers felt about the channel. The magic of the music video was that most viewers had never seen their musical heroes in live motion. They had only heard the music; they had never seen the music. All the attention paid to the visual appeal of music stars had changed the ways artists had to market themselves: "Not until the creation of MTV in 1981 did a Hollywood sensibility enter the world of music . . . pop personalities are now under pressure to correct their physical appearances to fit current notions of what is acceptable. The out of shapers don't have a chance."[21] When watching a selection of Bon Jovi videos, one can see how their sense of appearance changed over the years. By the release of the third album, *Slippery When Wet*, and the first video off the album, "You Give Love a Bad Name," the stylistic cohesiveness of the band had been honed into a "look."

In addition to fashion and youth culture, MTV also had an interdependent relationship with film. Once it became evident that music videos were an enterprise in which investors and record companies were willing to pay big money, talented individuals signed on to direct them. Some very successful movie directors got their start directing music videos for MTV. A few include David Fincher (*Fight Club, Panic Room, The Social Network*), Spike Jonze (*Being John Malkovich, Adaptation*), Michel Gondry (*Eternal Sunshine of the Spotless Mind, The Green Hornet*), and Michael Bay (*Armageddon, Pearl Harbor, Transformers*). *Footloose* and *Flashdance* are just two examples of hugely successful movies that are sometimes perceived as having been promoted as extended music videos. Some go so far as to suggest they were conceived as kind of an extended music video experience due to the fact that music is featured so predominantly in them. *Footloose* is a good example of a movie that integrated the music video culture into its production to great success. It has been mentioned in the press that Jon Bon Jovi was invited to audition for the lead role that eventually went to Kevin Bacon. The soundtrack of the movie was extremely popular, as was the film itself: "The movie 'Footloose' and its peppy soundtrack of high gloss junk-food songs represents a crossroads in the romance between Hollywood movies and pop records that began six years ago with 'Saturday Night Fever.' That romance has recently been given a fresh jolt of energy by the rise of music video. Suddenly, records, movies and video software have found themselves interrelated configurations of the same basic product."[22]

In the 1980s, Bon Jovi was the perfect band for MTV, and MTV was the perfect vehicle through which the band sold records. The camera and the girls loved Jon Bon Jovi. Once they found their video groove, their fun and relatable hooks and lyrics gave birth to irresistible videos. The band excelled in live performance, and the best videos of their career featured them performing live. Generation X was tuned in to their TVs without the Internet to distract them from catching their favorite artists' videos. Kids may have not been able to get to a Bon Jovi concert, but they could surely watch them perform on MTV. The music informed the videos and the videos perpetuated the coolness of the band. The images and ideology of the videos of Bon Jovi solidified a strong fan base that learned to love them through the medium of television. There are many artists who did very well on MTV: Michael Jackson, Madonna, Duran Duran, Van Halen, and Huey Lewis and the News; but Bon Jovi was the band that imprinted on a generation. MTV in the '80s has much to do with the fact that Bon Jovi later had the top-grossing tours in the industry, in 2008 and 2010. It seems as if Bon Jovi and MTV were made for each other. Without the popularity of the music video in the 1980s, Bon Jovi might not have cultivated the loyal fan base of kids (now in their forties) who continue to turn out for their concerts the world over.

Former Bongiovi family home as it is today in Sayreville, New Jersey.

Jon Bon Jovi's alma mater, Sayreville War Memorial High School, Sayreville, New Jersey.

Sayreville High School emblem.

The Soul Kitchen Restaurant in Red Bank, New Jersey.

The Soul Kitchen herb garden.

The garage of the FastLane where David Rashbaum used to park his van for rehearsals and performances.

The FastLane club as it appears today in Asbury Park, New Jersey.

The legendary Stone Pony club on the shore in Asbury Park, New Jersey.

4

EXCESS AND SOBRIETY

THE REAGANS AND THE "WAR ON DRUGS"

By the 1980s, the amount of drugs in the United States had increased significantly enough to warrant the government declaring a "war on drugs." Drugs had permeated every level of society in the United States and were pouring into the country at an unprecedented rate. During the eight years he was president, Ronald Reagan made the fight against illegal drugs a highlight of his administration, culminating in the signing of the Anti-Drug Abuse Act in 1986. President Reagan was not the first public official to use the phrase "war on drugs," but he was the first to fight against them in a high-profile manner. During his first term the First Lady, Nancy Reagan, also took up arms in the drug fight. The "Just Say No" campaign launched by Nancy Reagan in 1983 included commercial and print advertising; in addition, the First Lady visited many schools personally to spread her message. The campaign garnered mixed reviews, and, in retrospect, many health professionals think direct language about the dangers of drug use is more effective when talking to teens about drugs than a glib "just say no." In all fairness, many thought the campaign had strengths, and the concept was easy for young people to grasp. Adults today remember the campaign. The response of the presidential office, the president, and the First Lady to the drug culture demonstrated the seriousness of the biggest social issue of the day.

The music industry of the '80s was intimately affected by the drug culture in America. In the recent book titled *I Want My MTV* (2011), dozens of musicians and music industry professionals share stories of drug use and abuse in executive offices, backstage, and on the sets of music videos during the '80s. Throughout American history, beloved music artists have died from drug use and drug overdoses: Whitney Houston (cocaine); Michael Jackson (Propofol); Elvis Presley (prescription drugs); Janis Joplin (heroin); Hillel Slovak of the Red Hot Chili Peppers (heroin); and Shannon Hoon of Blind Melon (cocaine) are just a few. Of course, being a professional musician does not necessarily include drug use; however, there is no argument against the fact that the lifestyle as we know it caters to the indulgence of substances.

Behind the scenes of the '80s music industry was ever-present drug activity. *Rolling Stone* assistant editor Andy Greene said: "The Los Angeles scene was just like Rome at its peak—filled with debauchery. There were girls everywhere, drugs everywhere. It was the era of AIDS, and they were living like it wasn't."[1] The glam metal scene in Los Angeles was particularly notorious for drug use, and the band Mötley Crüe was the poster child for it. Members of the band were notorious for debauched behavior. They decided to sell their tales in the recent biography *The Dirt: Confessions of the World's Most Notorious Rock Band*. The book chronicles behavior that included heroin and cocaine use, alcoholism, overdoses, rehabilitation attempts, vandalism, a DUI conviction that resulted in a death, the debasement of women, and all kinds of abhorrent acts. Mötley Crüe was under the same management as Bon Jovi during the '80s, although they were, and are, very different bands.

Another metal band that peaked in the '80s was Van Halen. Metal contemporaries of Bon Jovi and Mötley Crüe, Van Halen had been on the professional music scene ten years longer than the other two bands. Anchored by brothers Alex and Eddie Van Halen, the band has been known for substance abuse problems. The fact that they are currently enjoying a successful world tour and are still alive is miraculous. A 2008 interview with sometime lead singer Sammy Hagar revealed that "there was always substance abuse in the band."[2] Hagar shared his opinion that "Eddie's problems are all from drugs and alcohol, and all of it self-inflicted. Eddie's not tortured by anything but Eddie."[3] One former band member writing a memoir about his days in the band is a recurring theme in the music industry.

In Guns N' Roses' former drummer's autobiography *My Appetite for Destruction* (2011), Steven Adler describes his own severe drug addiction and that of his band mates. Unfortunately, Adler's story is not that uncommon among rock stars of the '80s. History has shown that an indulgence in drugs during a band's popularity in the '80s can lead to a lifetime of struggle to overcome serious addiction. In the past few years, Steven Adler has appeared on Dr. Drew Pinsky's popular show *Celebrity Rehab*.

The '80s were known as the decade of cocaine, but socially, Americans had not come to terms with what drug addiction could do to a life. People seemed to have an attitude toward cocaine in the '80s similar to the attitude people had toward smoking cigarettes in the '50s: no big deal. Former MTV video producer and executive Sharon Oreck recalls the attitude: "In the early '80s, there was still this bizarre impression that heroin was a drug, but cocaine was like a cigarette. Pretty much every person in the music-video industry was doing cocaine, except me. And I wasn't doing cocaine only because I'd finished with it in the '70s. It was beyond pervasive. Everyone was high. I never heard the term 'rehab' until 1985 or so. And then, all of a sudden, I started hearing it a lot."[4] Perhaps the music executives and producers looked the other way while artists were using drugs because they knew it fueled them and gave them energy to work longer than they should. There may have been a line of thinking that cocaine inspired creative ideas. Certainly people would not have taken so much of it if it did not make them feel good. Either way, it was not only the musicians doing drugs. Popular video director Wayne Isham shared that he cannot believe that he, and the musicians, did so many drugs and were still able to work and finish videos.[5] Tommy Lee recalls the special relationship his band had with Isham: "Whatever we were doing, Wayne Isham was doing. If we were partying, he was partying. If we were doing drugs, he was doing drugs. He'd wake up at 8 AM, hung-over, and direct the video. He was like the fifth Beatle."[6]

Not every artist was indulging in drug use. Singer Melba Moore was one of the first music celebrities to speak out about the dangers of drugs, in an article in the industry's *Billboard* magazine. She asked that other musicians participate in benefits across the country to aid local communities. Bon Jovi would later follow her example, as would other bands, MTV, and the music industry.

BON JOVI'S EARLY DAYS

There is practically nothing known by the general public about Bon Jovi's drug use in their early career. Unlike Mötley Crüe, the band does not tell tales of any kind. Of course, one reason may be that there is nothing to tell, but considering the time and place, that is not likely. By all accounts, Bon Jovi has been a professional operation from day one. They show up on time and play a great show. Only the people who were there know what really happened. There have been a few rumors. Former tour manager Rich Bozzett released a trashy exposé in 2010 that alleges that some of the band members used drugs on an airplane during the '80s. He also claims that Jon Bon Jovi used amphetamines before shows to increase his energy level. Adam Curry of MTV fame alleges that Jon Bon Jovi once traveled with his own doctor, who gave Halcion to anyone who wanted it.[7] Jon Bon Jovi himself stated in a *People* magazine interview that he was into drugs "very young" and let it go "very young." Whether or not "very young" means his teen years or twenties is speculative. He goes on to explain that he does not believe he could handle any kind of drug use and realized this at an early age.[8] Considering his track record, this is most likely true. Today, he appears to live the life of an exemplary family man and honest citizen. Jon Bon Jovi has not shown up to interviews stoned or drunk, he has not trashed property, he has not been convicted for a DUI, and he does not end up in the press for drug-related activities. He runs a huge business (Bon Jovi) and a philanthropic organization (Philadelphia Soul Foundation, Soul Kitchen) and has a large family.

As for the rest of the band, executives, and crew, it is impossible to know exactly what went on in regard to drug use. It is probably to the band's advantage that the '80s was a very different time when it came to technology. It was not as easy to take pictures or record video. When people were bored, they could not post to social networking sites; in short, there was much more privacy. Unlike today, then it was possible to get away with bad behavior without being recorded in some way. Recently, England's Prince Harry was a victim of modern technology on a trip to Las Vegas, where a cell phone took a picture that was less than royal.

All the members of the band have spoken publicly about the fact that they were very "burned out" and "wasted" toward the end of the New Jersey Tour in 1988. They had been touring two huge albums relentlessly, and the pace was almost manic. Drug use may, or may not, have contributed to the exhaustion and apathy that almost led to the demise of the band. After a hiatus and realignment of goals, they got back together and continued their career.

One notorious event that occurred in the band's early years was their trip to Russia as part of the Moscow Music Peace Festival. Held in August of 1989, the event was conceived of and created by their manager at the time, Doc McGhee, as a kind of homage to the Woodstock tradition. He took all the bands he was managing at the time to Moscow, Russia, for a once-in-a-lifetime rock concert. Bon Jovi, Mötley Crüe, Skid Row, the Scorpions, Cinderella, and Ozzy Osbourne all went. The purpose of the festival was to raise money for anti-alcohol and anti-drug organizations, so it was expected that all the bands performing would be sober. Apparently it did not play out that way. Tommy Lee of Mötley Crüe: "It was all bad from the moment we stepped on the plane. We had a pact as a band that we were going to stay sober . . . there was a so-called doctor on board, who was plying the bands who weren't sober with whatever medicine they needed. It was clear that this was going to be a monumental festival of hypocrisy."[9] The event was historically significant in that it was the first Western rock concert of its kind. Over one hundred thousand people were in attendance, and video of the event looks like a Western rock concert. The audience was not seated but standing, and there were even handmade signs like the ones seen in Bon Jovi videos. By all accounts, what happened onstage was a big success. What happened after the concert is another story. According to Tommy Lee, when he saw the pyrotechnics that Bon Jovi had for their set, he was livid, and fired Doc McGhee on the spot. Mötley Crüe had specifically been told that they could not have pyro effects during their set because of permits, and they were angry that Bon Jovi, a band they did not respect, had these effects. Apparently, Mötley Crüe refused to fly home to the United States on the same plane as Doc McGhee, and their business relationship was over.

It is most likely that some of the drama surrounding the Moscow Peace Festival had to do with drug use, but the bands involved were able to deliver where it counted—onstage. In video coverage of the event, Russian youth are clearly ecstatic and having a great time at the concert. The event probably did more for United States–Russia relations than any formal political event ever had. Jon explained his expectations for the event versus the reality:

> When we played Lenin Stadium where our Olympic athletes could not go . . . we realized that though they hadn't been exposed to pop culture . . . their vision and version of it was alive in their minds and in their hearts. They embraced us with that same curiosity that we embraced them . . . if you would see the Soviet infrastructure like I saw it at that time you would shake your head and say "these are the bad guys?"[10]

MAKE A DIFFERENCE FOUNDATION

Bon Jovi's first manager, Doc McGhee, was an ambitious, up-and-coming music executive when he met the band in 1983. He was smart enough to sell himself to Jon Bon Jovi, and beat out several more seasoned professionals for the job as the band's manager. He was also involved in drug trafficking. It is impossible to know whether Bon Jovi had knowledge of his illegal activities. Tommy Lee has described an incident in the Cayman Islands when McGhee's activities raised the suspicion of authorities: "One time these killer blonds came down from New Orleans and kicked it with Doc, Leigh, and the guys from Bon Jovi, who Doc was also managing . . . Leigh taped drugs all over their bodies and dropped them off at the airport . . . they found the coke. . . . they knew the girls were with Leigh and the Bon Jovi guys, who had left the island on the previous flight."[11] Bon Jovi's flight was then called back to the island to be searched. No one in Bon Jovi was arrested, but McGhee's activities put the band in some precarious situations.

What is known for sure is that in 1989, after Doc McGhee was convicted of smuggling several tons of marijuana into North Carolina, Jon Bon Jovi put his organization on the line in order to keep McGhee out of prison. He offered the band's services and participation in various anti-drug activities that were part of McGhee's probation package.

McGhee started the Make a Difference Foundation as an umbrella organization under which he could perform anti-drug outreach activities. One of those activities was a visit by Jon Bon Jovi to Raleigh, North Carolina's Broughton High School to talk to the students about the dangers of drugs. The most significant work of the Foundation was the previously mentioned Moscow Peace Festival in 1989. McGhee's prison-free sentence is a reflection of Bon Jovi's popularity at the time. It is also a high-profile example of the importance of loyalty in the Bon Jovi organization. Jon Bon Jovi, and the whole band, took a significant risk in supporting Doc McGhee. They stood by McGhee and they stayed with him (for a while).

THE BAND AND SUBSTANCE ABUSE

When bassist Alec John Such left the band in the mid-1990s, Bon Jovi divulged nothing to the media about the reasons for his departure. Since he had been an equal member of the band throughout their two biggest albums and tours and was genuinely liked by the band, the firing seems odd. One explanation is that he had a substance abuse problem and was not able to perform at his best. This is pure conjecture, but the most likely reason. By all accounts Such was an accomplished musician and stage personality. In a rare moment, Jon discussed Such's exit from the band: "Alec Such was the first rock star in the band . . . he looked the part, he sang great. He was crazy as the day was long. He pulled a gun on me . . . I've lived it. But while we were all young, dumb, and havin' fun, we started to get very serious about it and we were five albums in and . . . he couldn't even play on them. . . . He knew that we were . . . I let him go." Jon goes on to explain that he is grateful that Alec never wrote a book or "told tales in the media." He claims the reason the band never replaced Such is because they memorialize his role and remember him being there in the beginning.[12]

Richie Sambora and Tico Torres have both spoken publicly about their addictions. While they are both sober now, there have been close calls and troubles in the past. In April of 2011, Sambora left a world tour to go to rehab. The band did not stop performances but enlisted professional guitarist Phil Xenidis to stand in for Sambora. There were raised eyebrows from fans and the media at the band's decision to keep going, but the band wanted to keep their commitments. The public image suggested they'd had enough and were not going to stop the train of a worldwide tour for Sambora. This reality was probably a great motivator for Sambora to get well and reclaim his position in the band. Bon Jovi backup stalwart bassist Hugh McDonald and guitarist Bobby Bandiera were also on hand to help fill in Sambora's absence. Richie has had other troubles in the past. He was arrested on a DUI charge in California in 2008, while driving his daughter and her friend. This arrest came less than a year after his previous rehab stay in 2007. Sambora's ex-wife and the mother of his daughter, Heather Locklear, has also had public struggles with substances. In January of 2012, Locklear was hospitalized for complications from prescription drug and alcohol use.

In the band's 2009 documentary *When We Were Beautiful*, Richie Sambora openly talked about his substance abuse issues: "I was going through such a dark period . . . physically I was shaky, I was not well and emotionally, I was not well . . . I thought I was getting through . . . I had broken my arm and the pain pills started, the boozin', and all that . . . I was kinda gone, you know? . . . It was life just mounting up on me . . . I was killing myself slowly, but that's not the way to live."[13]

Bon Jovi drummer Tico Torres revealed himself as a recovering alcoholic in *When We Were Beautiful*. He credits playing golf and making art for helping him stay sober. He has said: "I was killing myself with drinking years ago. I was the kind of person who wouldn't drink for months and then just load off two bottles." Jon Bon Jovi said the following about Torres in 2009: "He had a lot of demons . . . he was a really bad drunk . . . 'T' was a very mean, mean man. He'd get in a lot of trouble with a lot of people. But, fortunately, his is the most together life of all of ours."[14]

There is relatively little published about Torres's personal life or issues. In older candid pictures of the band, he is almost always holding a drink. He is currently on his third marriage and has a son. Torres has found a philosophy that works for him: "I've learned to live in the present more than anything, forget the past, and I don't even think about the future."[15]

There is no question that Bon Jovi has survived the drugs aspect of the rock and roll lifestyle much better than most. They have seen friends and colleagues lose their careers, and lives, over substance abuse. After some well-hidden wild behavior in their early days, they have managed to keep a very professional image in their later years. The fact that Sambora knows he has to go to rehab as soon as he starts drinking should be considered a sign of strength—he knows his limitations and wants to stay sober. The fact that three of the four band members are divorced may or may not have anything to do with substance abuse. Chances are, for Sambora and Torres, it does. Jon Bon Jovi's longtime marriage to Dorothea Hurley, his committed family life, and his philanthropic work go a very long way in stabilizing and enforcing the image of Bon Jovi despite his colleagues' substance issues.

5

CROSS-COMMERCIALISM AS A SURVIVAL TOOL

TELEVISION

In the 21st century, television continues to be the dominant advertising vehicle for all things commercial, including music. In the spring of 2012, and for the first time, Jon Bon Jovi endorsed a product by appearing in a television commercial. The product was Advil, and Jon claimed that he needed it sometimes to help him keep up with his hectic schedule. In the commercial, Jon sits at a table in his own Soul Kitchen restaurant, speaking casually to the camera as if addressing a good friend: "Pain doesn't have much of a place in my life. I checked the schedule and it's not on it."[1] Clearly, the makers of Advil thought he could sell their product, and he probably has; moreover, because Jon has not appeared in any other commercial in the United States, his endorsement carries more credibility.

In a *Forbes* interview, Brian Groves, vice president and chief marketing officer of U.S. Consumer Healthcare at Pfizer, explained why the drug company chose Jon Bon Jovi for their campaign: "Jon is an authentic American icon, as is Advil, and Jon's brand, in his entertainment life and his business and philanthropy, appears very focused on solving problems and getting right to the point and that's how we feel about Advil."[2]

The first person to come to mind to sell an analgesic may not be Jon Bon Jovi, but he is speaking to his peer group, which is approaching late middle life. More than one person probably had to look twice at the television screen when the commercial came on, to assure himself that he was seeing one of his favorite rock stars selling Advil. In the previously mentioned interview, Groves revealed that the Pfizer financially supports the Jon Bon Jovi Soul Foundation.

This was not the first time a celebrity endorsed and appeared in commercials for a product. The American public has seen everything from Jamie Lee Curtis selling yogurt that regulates digestion (Activia) to William Shatner promoting low travel prices (Priceline) to country music star Garth Brooks selling soda (Dr. Pepper). What they have not seen is a popular rock star selling a commonly used product. Why does Jon Bon Jovi need to do a commercial? It is most likely that he thought the appearance would serve his career in some direct way. One reason may be that the commercial would run when Bon Jovi was not on tour, thereby keeping him in the public eye. Maybe highly paid statisticians told him that his age group uses Advil and most of the people who attend his concerts would notice the commercial and remember they liked him. Whatever the reason for Jon Bon Jovi appearing in a commercial for a consumer product, it was no doubt motivated by his personal business goals. The choice to do a commercial makes him unique among his peer group (whether this unique status is positive or negative is up to personal interpretation). He has managed to appear regularly on national television, speaking directly to an audience. He is promoting Advil, but is also promoting himself and his band.

Since 1971, *Saturday Night Live* (*SNL*) has been a cornerstone of American television. The enormously popular show stays relevant with its weekly guest star (one of the hottest actors of the moment), its larger-than-life repeat hosts (Alec Baldwin, Steve Martin, Tom Hanks), and the weekly musical guest. Sometimes the host and musical guest are the same. Over the years, Bon Jovi has appeared several times on *SNL* as musical guest to promote their albums and tours, and in October 2007, Jon Bon Jovi appeared as combined actor/host and musical guest.

SNL likes to have some fun with their guest stars. An actor's current hit show or most notorious film role are always fodder for the *SNL* writers. Jon Bon Jovi was no exception, although his skits were not about his acting but his music career. His graciousness in poking fun at himself indicates a person comfortable in his own skin. One skit from the show presents a fictional 1983 Bon Jovi sitting around in a rehearsal space in New Jersey, questioning why the band is required to have the name Bon Jovi. Jon eventually concedes that in twenty-five years he will change the band name to Sambora or Torres. A second skit imagines what has probably been many a young woman's fantasy. A teenage Amy Poehler is in her bedroom, where a life-size poster of Jon Bon Jovi hangs adoringly on the back of her bedroom door. While wishing out loud that she could go to the Cinderella/Bon Jovi concert that night, Jon materializes out of thin air. He tells Amy that she will grow up one day and have everything she wants. He is a monument to his 1980s persona, wearing stonewashed jeans, a duster coat, a ripped T-shirt, and tousled hair. He is an intact 1980s Jon Bon Jovi. It is interesting to consider what motivation Jon Bon Jovi had for poking fun at his 1980s persona. Most men of his wealth and position would not want to portray themselves as anything less than current and now. Maybe he did it so his children could get a feeling of what the '80s were about for him. Perhaps he wanted to remind his fans of the '80s heyday. Most likely the *SNL* writers wanted to give Bon Jovi fans a retrospective of the band as well as a current look. Another skit from 2001 features Jon and Richie conducting dance auditions for their upcoming tour. They calmly observe *SNL* cast members performing interpretive dances to "Runaway" and "It's My Life." It is clear that the guys are having fun.

The band made a musical guest appearance in 2009 to promote their album *The Circle*. Bon Jovi has made more appearances on *SNL* in the third decade of their career than the first, a testament to the commercially savvy tactics of Jon Bon Jovi. Their point is not to make long-term fans happy that their favorite band is on *SNL*; their point is to gain new fans. The show is typically watched by a younger viewing demographic, who may or may not be familiar with Bon Jovi. The band is in fact introducing themselves to younger generations through their musical performances on the show, while at the same time educating them about the history of the band through the skits. All this results in a public relations double whammy that fits neatly into an hour-and-a-half time slot. *SNL* is a show that feeds the water cooler talk at the office on Monday morning. It is one of the only live television shows that people watch at the same time. It is a common denominator in the vast choice of television programming we have today. For Bon Jovi, it has been a marketing tool to keep them in the conversation with trendy actors and musicians.

NBC is not the only television network to feature Bon Jovi. CBS and *Sunday Night Football* collaborated with the band to use "This Is Our House" as the show's theme song. The affiliation with the football franchise is a shrewd move that proves Jon Bon Jovi feels comfortable in the arena of professional sports and intends to stay. The feel-good, fun times anthem "This Is Our House" strengthens the connection between manly sports and Bon Jovi every time the song is played, reminding the audience that Bon Jovi is still relevant in their lives.

Bon Jovi is featured somewhat regularly on the entertainment news shows such as *Entertainment Tonight*, *TMZ*, and *Extra*. The coverage increases when they are on tour. In recent years, much of the media attention has been devoted to the demise of the marriage of Richie Sambora and Heather Locklear and the role of Denise Richards in the divorce.

Sambora's and Locklear's substance issues, arrests, and traffic violations have been covered heavily. No publicity is bad publicity in terms of keeping Bon Jovi in the forefront of popular culture. It's a true shame that most of the good works of the band go ignored in the press, but rehabilitation stints, traffic violations, and family feuds are featured whenever possible. The press offered a skewed view; for example, in 2011, when Richie Sambora checked himself into rehab in the middle of a tour, the press covered the event with the zealousness of a presidential election, with questions like "Is Bon Jovi over?" "Was Richie Sambora fired?" "Will fans ask for ticket refunds?" In the end it all worked out, with Sambora joining the tour again as soon as he was able. The fact that Richie Sambora was able to drum up that level of interest from the press is significant. The media was not able to resist pointing out that Sambora was in trouble and going to rehab again. Almost every major media outlet mentioned that Sambora was leaving the tour and why. The tone of the coverage was almost gleeful instead of empathetic. Instead of pointing out that Sambora was doing the right thing by addressing his issues head-on, the press moved on to speculation about the demise of the band.

The media's treatment of Sambora's addiction issues speaks to a larger issue in American culture. Americans care about what mistakes celebrities make. We like to see celebrities stumble and fall. Public humiliation is expected and relished. This phenomenon has been in existence since the beginning of celebrity status.

Richie Sambora has also enjoyed positive television coverage. In 2012 he appeared on television as the guest band leader for the *Late Late Show with Craig Ferguson* on CBS. Sambora has said he was inspired by the stint John Lennon did on *The Mike Douglas Show* in 1972.

Because of Jon Bon Jovi's significant financial success, philanthropic works, and various franchises, he has been a guest on many of the high-brow talk shows, like *Oprah*, *Larry King Live*, *Person of Interest* on CBS, and so on. His unprecedented, $1 million donation to Oprah's Angel Network ensured him a special place in her pantheon of celebrities. Several years later she selected him as a subject of her *Master Class* series on the Oprah Winfrey Network (OWN).

It is not possible to overestimate the long-reaching influence of Oprah Winfrey. All the celebrities who have appeared on her show over the years, with a couple of exceptions, have been Oprah-approved. If Oprah loved a celebrity and thought he was worthy, the studio audience loved him; therefore, the viewers at home loved him. He would almost become Oprah's friend. Jon Bon Jovi was, and is, definitely a member of this exclusive club. His appearance on Oprah's *Master Class* series puts him in the same category as Sidney Poitier, Jane Fonda, Maya Angelou, Diane Sawyer, and Condoleezza Rice, among others. The fact that Jon agreed to the in-depth interview indicates his deep regard for Oprah. He obviously felt he had some wisdom to pass on at that point in his career. The fact that he is taken seriously in this regard by viewers and is included in this elite celebrity pack is proof that he still has relevance as a celebrity. His point of view, for better or worse, continues to influence the discussion of music and cultural issues in American and world culture.

Despite all the media and television coverage, there are very few in-depth, one-on-one interviews with members of the band. CBS's *60 Minutes* did one in-depth interview in 2008. Filmed at the New Jersey home of Jon Bon Jovi, the episode included a sit-down interview as well as an extensive tour of the house and grounds. These types of interviews are somewhat rare. Most of the time when Bon Jovi appears on television, the feature gives a perfunctory and fleeting glance.

In 2009, Jon Bon Jovi took the concept of using television as an advertising vehicle to an entirely new level when he signed an exclusive deal with NBC Universal. Basically, he committed Bon Jovi to only appearing on NBC or its subsidiaries for the two-month period of November and December 2009. During this time he appeared on the *Today Show*, *The Tonight Show with Jay Leno*, *NBC Nightly News*, and *Saturday Night Live*. The band also appeared on *Inside the Actors Studio* on NBC Universal channel Bravo. Former Bon Jovi music manager Jack Rovner worked with NBC head Jeff Zucker to secure the deal. Jon Bon Jovi was promoted as NBC's "Artist in Residence."

This unprecedented arrangement with a major television network was as carefully manufactured as a United Nations peace agreement. While the exclusive deal was advertised in press releases, it is doubtful most of the general public knew of the arrangement (the average TV viewer may have noticed that Bon Jovi seemed to be on the screen more than usual). This move utilized the concept of cross-commercialism in a brilliant way. The variety of programming covered several demographics of watchers. The programming covered the late-night audiences and the early-morning viewers as well as the viewers who enjoyed more offbeat shows like *Inside the Actors Studio*.

AWARDS SHOWS

Awards shows have long been a staple of celebrities. It is possible to regard an awards show as an extended commercial. An awards show promotes celebrities and their work and reminds the audience to go to the movies, buy the album, watch the show, and on and on. It is not a secret that those in a position to critique Bon Jovi's music have not usually been favorable. Throughout their career there have been very few big awards and only one Grammy win (the "Who Says You Can't Go Home" collaboration with Jennifer Nettles).

Bon Jovi knows what is required of them as professionals and has made the rounds of the various awards shows. The band members have appeared on most of the major music awards shows, including the MTV American and European Music Awards, My VH1 Music Awards, People's Choice Awards, Grammy Awards, American Music Awards, Academy of Country Music Awards, Billboard Music Awards, and many more. Like Bruce Springsteen, Paul McCartney, Billy Joel, Elton John, and others, the members of Bon Jovi are starting to take on the roles of elder statesmen at these shows. They have had a career longer than some music artists honored have been alive. Even if they do not win an award, it is worth their time to appear on the show to promote an album and to remind audiences of previous hits.

Jon Bon Jovi's and Richie Sambora's 2009 induction into the Songwriters Hall of Fame was a major coup in their career. It is probably the most prestigious recognition they have received from the professional music world. The fortieth-anniversary induction and concert featured fellow inductees Crosby, Stills and Nash and musical theater composer Stephen Schwartz, among others. To receive this recognition at this point in their career is an affirmation of Bon Jovi's staying power. Many of the 2009 inductees are not nearly as active professionally as Bon Jovi. Case in point: Crosby, Stills and Nash; Felix Cavaliere; and James Rado. Bon Jovi is a band that the year before grossed more on their tour than any other musical act in the world! Whether the Songwriters honor speaks more to their early work or their overall body of work is somewhat irrelevant in light of the fact that a band that formed in 1983 was the top touring act in the world in 2008.

In 2010, Bon Jovi was nominated for the Rock and Roll Hall of Fame but not inducted. Known around the world as the top honor for musical artists, the organization has expanded its definition of rock. Inductees represent genres of music such as rap, rhythm and blues, country, soul, acoustic, heavy metal, alternative, etc. Despite the new inclusive culture of the Hall, a cloud of controversy usually hangs over whatever inductees are nominated or chosen. People always feel someone worthy was left out or the wrong person was selected. Some wonder how organized the process is, and the degree to which someone is considered a "real musician" creates considerable debate among musical peers. Bon Jovi is still waiting.

MUSIC AND PERFORMANCE

Of course, the chief commercial enterprise of any band is selling records. The band's record sales are estimated to be one hundred twenty-five million albums and counting. There are very few bands in the

20th/21st century who have matched Bon Jovi's sales records; Bon Jovi's sales put the band in the same category as Bruce Springsteen, Chicago, the Eagles, and Garth Brooks. *Billboard* ranked them the ninth-highest-grossing touring artist of the 2000s.[3] One unique aspect of the creative life of Bon Jovi is the breadth and length of their discography. The simple fact that it spans thirty years is significant. That is enough time for two generations of fans to form a relationship with the band and their musical output. For example, people who were teens in the '80s and grew up with the band fondly remember the albums *Slippery When Wet* and *New Jersey*. In their twenties, these same fans discovered a 2.0 version of the band in the '90s with *Keep the Faith*. They enjoyed *Crush* as thirty-somethings, and moved on with more mature albums like *Lost Highway* and *The Circle* as forty-somethings in the 2000s.

Bon Jovi's discography begins with *Bon Jovi* in 1984 and is still growing. It is impossible to disregard the level of determination it takes to change with the music industry and stay relevant as a band. With the exception of a long hiatus before *Keep the Faith*, Bon Jovi has been writing, recording, and/or touring albums for the past thirty years. The core of the band's career has been their discography and relentless touring, but there is no doubt that each step has been carefully planned and executed. By showing the public only what they want us to see, Bon Jovi has crafted a brand that has stood the test of time.

Bon Jovi was one of the first rock bands to understand the crucial need for international touring. From the early tours to Japan and Russia to Abu Dhabi in 2009, they have covered the continents. This approach has revolutionized the music industry the world over. Many touring acts have come to see the value in an international presence and followed Bon Jovi's example. Occasional tours to faraway places increase interest in future tours and boost ticket sales. The tour is also a kind of insurance policy for album sales. For example, if the album does not do well in the United States, maybe people in Australia will like it, and it will make money.

One benefit of a sizeable discography is that less commercially successful works do not have as much of a negative impact. Bon Jovi's big hits have allowed them to take certain risks artistically but not suffer financially. Not many bands with a successful songwriting strategy try a renegade move in the middle of their career, but Bon Jovi did. Their

2003 album, titled *The Left Feels Right: Greatest Hits with a Twist*, took daring strides away from the winning Bon Jovi formula for hits. The band took existing songs, reformatted the arrangements and instrumentation, and recorded them. The result is a kind of disconcerting, off-balance album. It is hard to get comfortable listening to "Livin' on a Prayer" as a ballad if you know the original version. After playing those hits thousands of times, new arrangements were undoubtedly interesting for Bon Jovi to play, but the average Bon Jovi fan did not respond well. Jon Bon Jovi talked about what it was like to be on the receiving end of that response in 2009's *When We Were Beautiful* documentary: "I tried to play what interested me; they hated it. I liked it, but they hated it."[4]

Another departure from the norm for the band was 2008's *Lost Highway* album. Taking a big artistic and creative risk, the band surrounded themselves with the best producers, advisers, and instrumentalists money could buy to record the album in a Nashville recording studio. With *Lost Highway*, the band embraced the country genre without losing the Bon Jovi style. Slickly produced, the flavor of the music is definitely Bon Jovi, and the country influences are deftly woven throughout the album. The result is much more successful than the *Left Feels Right* release. Popular collaborations with successful country stars Jennifer Nettles and LeAnn Rimes legitimized the band's relevance to country music. In the past, Jon has described the album as country-influenced rather than country. Either way, the risk paid off. The combination of fun, upbeat tunes and lyrical ballads, the popularity of the duet with Jennifer Nettles, and the enthusiasm of the band resulted in a new demographic of fans who might have never given Bon Jovi a listen if they did not hear the word "country" associated with the album.

There are very few music groups that have pulled off a genre switch like this one in the middle of their career. Perhaps the glossy new image of country music as more progressive and diverse tempted the band to give it a try. Country music has come a long way in the last thirty years. Musical acts are more diverse, and women especially have offered a more modern view than in years past. The average country fan is harder to pin down than she used to be. People from many socioeconomic classes enjoy country music.

One cross-commercial tactic of Bon Jovi is to make friends with younger artists. While some of their relationships with these artists are surely authentic friendships, it seems that some of them are meant for public consumption. Performances or associations with these artists immediately raise the band's cache with the younger population, as the band is seen as more relevant to their lives. By breaking out of their comfort zone, Bon Jovi raises their own awareness of current trends in the music business. A mention in the news of "Bon Jovi's performance with Rihanna last night" is sure to raise a few eyebrows.[5] The mention will also make people want to know more about how that came about. Rihanna produced her own commercial when she tweeted about her performance with Bon Jovi in Madrid. She performed "Livin' on a Prayer" with them as a surprise onstage in Madrid in conjunction with the 2010 MTV Europe Music Awards. YouTube clips are still available online.

Another one of Bon Jovi's popular younger friends is Kid Rock. Kid was featured in another surprise performance in concert with Bon Jovi in Detroit. He joined them onstage for a rendition of "Dead or Alive," to great appreciation from the audience. He later joined the band for a series of shows during their London stay at the O2 theater on The Circle Tour. Kid also appears briefly in the documentary *When We Were Beautiful*, talking about the relevancy of Bon Jovi. He mentions that with a song like "Livin' on a Prayer," the "song is bigger than the trend."[6]

American Idol (premiering in 2002) has put the music recording industry in every living room across the globe. What used to take place behind the closed doors of a music executive's office is now played out on a reality television show. Viewers vote for whom they consider the best, much like Romans cheered for gladiators back in the day. Considering the popularity and breadth of the show, it is not surprising that Jon Bon Jovi would become involved in some way.

In 2008, Bon Jovi took up-and-comer and *American Idol* star Chris Daughtry on the Lost Highway Tour as his opening act. It was a good choice, since Daughtry was enormously popular at the time. The relationship with Daughtry was also extremely fruitful for the band because his fan base was built from his appearances on *American Idol*, and his base at that time was much younger than the typical adult attending a Bon Jovi concert. Chris Daughtry had performed Bon Jovi's song "Dead or Alive" on an episode of *American Idol*, and Jon Bon Jovi eventually appeared on the show himself. The whole business was another public relations coup for Bon Jovi. By utilizing the talents of Chris Daughtry, they affiliated themselves with the most popular music show on television and put themselves directly in the middle of the popular music scene in America.

When touring, Bon Jovi will often offer an opportunity to young local bands to perform as their opening act. Typically, there will be some kind of contest coordinated with local media (radio stations, print media), and the winning band will headline Bon Jovi's show in their town. Of course, the performance is a huge opportunity for the winning band, who are ecstatic to find themselves performing in a huge arena. The setup gives Bon Jovi certain advantages, as well. They do not have to tour with the same opening act for months at a time, eliminating the possibility of backstage drama or competitive egos. They come off as heroes to the younger bands, which are desperate for exposure and could not dream of the kind of gigs Bon Jovi does all the time. It also connects the Bon Jovi brand with the hottest bands on the local markets. Leading up to a performance, kids in Anywhere, USA, hear the name of their favorite local band in tandem with Bon Jovi several times a day on the radio. They may even attend the show to see their favorite band and stick around to check out Bon Jovi. By using local talent as the opening act at their shows, Bon Jovi sells tickets, gains new fans, does good, and comes off as heroes. Brilliant.

There are very few venues that most music stars really want to play, and Central Park in the summer is one of them. Since the late 1960s it has been the venue of choice for the huge pop concert. The concerts that Diana Ross and Barbra Streisand (A *Happening in Central Park* live album) performed there helped to define their careers. When Bon Jovi had the opportunity to play a charity concert at Central Park, they took it. July 12, 2008, was the date of Bon Jovi's free concert in Central Park, New York City. *When We Were Beautiful* reveals Jon Bon Jovi discussing the stress of the situation. The concert was surrounded by legal issues with ticketing, and what had started out as a good deed ended up being quite complex. His perspective was that he was being punished for agreeing to do the free concert in the first place. Despite the behind-the-scenes drama, the event went off very well and drew capacity crowds. In a press conference before the show, Jon made sure to put the band's performance in context by stating that "this is the one the Beatles and the Rolling Stones never did."[7] Whenever he talked about the Central Park concert, especially to the press, he purposefully associated Bon Jovi with the other megastars who had performed there, like Luciano Pavarotti and Barbra Streisand. Jon Bon Jovi appears laid-back in interviews; however, there is almost a relentlessness in his up-selling of the band, which has paid off over the years. He is never off point. This is not merely conceit: it is advertising. Whatever the circumstances of the concert, Bon Jovi will always be included on the list of the few elite artists who had the opportunity to perform in the famous venue.

One lucrative cross-commercial opportunity for Bon Jovi has been the composition of music for film and television. Bon Jovi's version of the power ballad or the big rock anthem plays well in the film genre. The band's hits regularly turn up in films like *Rock Star*, *EDtv*, *Rock of Ages*, and countless others. Jon's album for *Young Guns II* certainly defined the film, with the power ballad "Blaze of Glory." The band's original songs appear in the films *Charlie's Angels*, *He's Just Not That Into You*, and *Armageddon* and on shows like *The Big Bang Theory*, *Glee*, *Dancing with the Stars*, and *The West Wing*.

MUSIC BUSINESS AND PUBLISHING

Most successful songwriters take some part in the publishing side of the music business. Not only did Bon Jovi eventually start publishing their own music, but they also were responsible for the development of other bands. Early in his career, Jon Bon Jovi realized he was in a position to help struggling bands, especially ones he knew from home. There has long been a rumor that he had a pact with friend Dave Sabo of Skid Row that whichever of them made it first would help the other. Jon made it, of course, and he did not forget his friend. In an excellent business move that took Skid Row from unknown band to hit maker and escalated Jon Bon Jovi to the role of business entrepreneur, he facilitated Skid Row's representation with his own manager, Doc McGhee, and established the Underground Music publishing company to promote their music.

Later in his career, Jon would fire Doc McGhee and take over control of all of the band's activities by establishing Bon Jovi Management. This business model has allowed Jon to pick and choose the people with whom he works in all aspects of music production, publishing, and touring and provides protection for the band, which works with only known entities. The team includes co-managers David Munns and Paul Korzilius, attorney Jerry Edelstein, and touring company AEG Live. The model that Jon created has protected the band and ensured its longevity.

In *When We Were Beautiful*, Jon Bon Jovi famously mentions that he is the "CEO of a large corporation."[8] This is most certainly true. In the world over there are very few performing artists who find themselves in Jon's position. The most common scenario is the music corporation handling the artist and telling him what to do. From the earliest days of rock and roll music touring (Elvis, Buddy Holly), corporate control has been the model. The Bon Jovi organization has turned this model on its head.

The documentary reveals much about the tour production itself. It gives an interesting insider's view into a world where millions of dollars are spent on glitzy aspects of production, like moving digital panels and multilevel movable stages; where hauling expensive gear in cargo planes all over the world is normal; and where hundreds of people depend on the work ethic of four guys for their livelihood and to support their own families.

It is also instructive to consider how much time, money, and effort is spent taking a rock concert on the road. It seems that even in countries of political unrest and relatively strict religious laws (United Arab Emirates and Ireland, for example), people will still come out for a concert. In the United States they will pay hundreds, even thousands of dollars for a premium ticket and a close look at their favorite band.

SOCIAL MEDIA

"Jon Bon Jovi is dead!" The news was all over Twitter on a Monday night in December 2011. Fortunately, it was not true. Jon Bon Jovi was only the latest celebrity to become the victim of a death hoax. Bon Jovi was actually trending for several hours ("trending" is when a word or phrase is one of the top ten terms mentioned on Twitter). For a certain generation Twitter is the news. The fact that Jon Bon Jovi was trending on the site speaks to his level of popularity.

With social media, this group of old-timers has unexpectedly mastered a commercial enterprise that didn't even exist for the first decade they were a band. No doubt Jon Bon Jovi recognized the benefit of having an online presence at all times; for example, the Bon Jovi website is like a commercial that never ends. Bon Jovi's Facebook page boasts almost eighteen million fans all over the globe. Who could see it coming? Yes, Bon Jovi tweets. If one is a fan who wants Bon Jovi on his phone, no problem. There is a Bon Jovi application with wallpaper, songs, pictures, and news to keep you informed twenty-four hours a day.

Bon Jovi's website, crafted by Bon Jovi Management, is comprehensive compared to other band websites. During tours, there is tour news, performance and interview videos, and ticket information. One can also find a biography of each band member and a complete band discography. There are links to the individual businesses of the band members. For $54.99, one can join "Backstage with Bon Jovi," with a basic membership that includes access to the forum pages, where fans post stories, pictures, videos, and just about everything having to do with the band. Upgraded membership packages are "Standard," $79.99, and "Signature," $159.99. Within the Backstage pages there is even BJTV (Bon Jovi Television), which features exclusive video clips of performances and interviews with the band. But wait! There's more! A Bon Jovi online store. One can own a hat, a T-shirt, underwear, jewelry, wrapping paper, a laptop cover, and countless other items imprinted with the Bon Jovi logo. The organization has claimed $2 million in merchandise sales off the website alone, not including merchandise sold on tour.[9]

Having an online presence is *de rigueur* for any public entity in the 21st century, whether it is a car company or a rock band. Instantaneous access to information is the new normal and is expected by fans. Bon Jovi has done more than most to integrate themselves into the online community and to develop their e-commerce business. The result is that fans (and anyone else) have access to a live presence online anytime. They can browse the Bon Jovi website, check their Twitter account, look up a forum or discussion group of interest, or even send emails to their favorite band member.

Bon Jovi even finds commercial opportunities when they don't go looking for them. The New Jersey tourism council came to the band for permission to use their song "Who Says You Can't Go Home."[10] They agreed to let the council use their song for a series of 2006 television commercials that promoted tourism in New Jersey. The fact that the tourism industry came to Jon Bon Jovi, and not Bruce Springsteen, is evidence that New Jersey may finally be taking some pride in their other son. The promotional campaign did more than just invite people to spend their tourism dollars in the Garden State. By using Bon Jovi's song, the council sent the message that Bon Jovi and New Jersey are one and the same. The advertising campaign was not an unprecedented move. Businesses that advertise have long engaged in the practice of searching for the perfect song or musical theme to help sell their project. The practice is almost certainly never random. In the United States, where the public is privy to the most sophisticated selling techniques in the world, an advertising campaign's song is chosen with a specific intent and purpose. One notable example is Nike's 1987 commercial, which sent a charge through the advertising and music worlds. The commercial featured the Beatles' song "Revolution." The publishing rights had been purchased for a quarter of a million dollars, but not from the Beatles; Michael Jackson owned the rights.

COMMERCIAL OPPORTUNITIES FOR THE BAND AS INDIVIDUALS

One aspect of Bon Jovi that makes them unique as a band, as well as entrepreneurs, is that they have aggressively pursued individual careers—in some cases, such as David Bryan, Richie Sambora, and Jon Bon Jovi, very public careers. The individual pursuits they have each undertaken include commercial and philanthropic interests. These paths have enabled the band to have their hands in many aspects of public life and culture, including musical theater, movies, television, solo albums, fashion, art, guitar design, professional football, golf, education, and dozens of philanthropic issues (to be discussed in a later chapter).

The members of Bon Jovi have never been ones to sit around and wait for opportunities to come to them. Without fail, each of them has rigorously pursued his own interests, businesses, and commercial enterprises. The time between the release of *New Jersey* (1988) and *Keep the Faith* (1992) was the first period of real individual development for the band. Subsequent hiatuses have provided other opportunities for the band to pursue activities that have nothing to do with Bon Jovi directly. From Richie Sambora working with the Les Paul or Marshall companies to Tico Torres displaying his art in a gallery, they each have found voices independent from the band.

Jon Bon Jovi

For the average person, a relationship is not usually a commercial opportunity for advancement. Celebrities often find their profile raised when they are dating another person who is famous, and the result is not always positive. Jon Bon Jovi was experiencing fame at an unprecedented level in the mid-1980s when he began dating the actress Diane Lane. As well-known as he was becoming, she was probably more well-known than he. Beautiful and individualistic, Lane was coming off big successes with movies like *The Cotton Club* and *The Outsiders*. She had been a child actor and already knew a lot about fame and Hollywood. Jon was in his first flush of huge fame and success. He had broken up with his high school girlfriend from Sayreville, Dorothea Hurley, and was out on the road most of the time. Diane Lane could not have been more different than Dorothea Hurley. Diane Lane had already experienced many of the things related to celebrity that Jon Bon Jovi was experiencing for the first time. With no responsibility of family on either side, their relationship mainly consisted of lots of photo opportunities and many glamorous episodes on the road. Being seen with Lane no doubt improved Bon Jovi's stature early in his career. This would not be the first time that one celebrity benefitted from the greater fame of another. It was his first successful cross-commercial campaign. Photographs of the couple, news clips, and print media all enforced the idea that Jon Bon Jovi had arrived. Eventually Jon and Diane broke up, and Jon got back together with Dorothea Hurley, whom he married in 1989. He has often made comments to the effect that he "tried the movie star girlfriend" and is very happy with his choice (no doubt Diane Lane has moved on as well). There has long been a rumor that the lyrics of "You Give Love a Bad Name" were inspired by Diane Lane. The rumor has never been confirmed by the band: "an angel's smile is what you sell, you promise me heaven then put me through hell."[11]

Just as Bon Jovi was settling into success, Jon Bon Jovi did something both unexpected and gutsy. He composed a solo album. When acquaintance Emilio Estevez approached Bon Jovi about composing a song or two for the movie *Young Guns II*, he got more than he expected. Bon Jovi offered to write an entire album of songs instead of just one or two. Whether it was artistic ambition or a business decision is hard to know. The result of his efforts was a Golden Globe Award from the Hollywood Foreign Press and a Grammy nomination in 1991 for Best Original Song, "Blaze of Glory." Jon also had his first, uncredited, professional film appearance in *Young Guns II* (there is a scene in which he is shot and falls into a pit). The title song off the album, "Blaze of Glory," was extremely popular and is still a favorite of fans today. This double whammy of group/band and solo success might have overwhelmed a lesser man, but Jon Bon Jovi took it all in stride. It is rather unusual for a member of a band to create a solo album so early in a band's career. The vast majority of musical artists who have done so have definitely not achieved the kind of commercial success Jon Bon Jovi did with "Blaze of Glory" (*Two Virgins* by John Lennon and Yoko Ono comes to mind). Some may look at the move as contrary to the interests of the rest of Bon Jovi, but the other band members have followed Jon's example over the years. Jon set the tone that individual pursuits were acceptable. In 2012, Jon added to his experience as a film composer by writing a few songs for the film *Stand Up Guys*, starring Al Pacino and Christopher Walken. The effort resulted in another Golden Globe nomination for Best Original Song, "Not Running Anymore."

There was much going on musically in America in the year 1992. U2 was in the midst of their Zoo TV Tour and R.E.M.'s big hit "Drive" was on the radio. Vocal group En Vogue released their second album, *Funky Divas*, and had two singles hit the top ten on the pop charts and number one on the R and B charts. k.d. lang's biggest hit, "Constant Craving," was on the charts. The biggest musical trend in 1992 was the full-blown emergence of grunge rock. All-male bands in shorts and flannel plaid shirts dominated the charts, and Kurt Cobain's groundbreaking band Nirvana broke the mold of popular music. Despite all this creative music activity, the biggest music news event of the year was Jon Bon Jovi cutting off his long hair. One has to wonder if a manager or publicist planted the seeds for this news item or if some eager journalist actually wrote up the story. Either way, the event had national news coverage. The interest in this story was proof that people found Bon Jovi and "hair band" synonymous.

Jon Bon Jovi had set out to conquer the world. Despite having a hugely successful music career, he decided he wanted to become a movie actor. Reflecting on his movie career, Jon has referred to himself as "the Tom Cruise of the music world and the Elvis Costello of the movie business."[12] He had commercial success in music, but not in movies. He had critical success as an actor in movies, but not critical success in music. Jon Bon Jovi is not the first recording artist to venture into the art of film acting. Elvis Presley, Frank Sinatra, and Whitney Houston are just a few singers/musicians who have translated their gifts to the silver screen (with varying degrees of success). Perhaps inspired by the time spent on the set of *Young Guns II*, Jon Bon Jovi began his pursuit of an acting career with formal study. He attended classes and coachings and went on auditions. His first major film role was 1995's *Moonlight and Valentino*, with Whoopi Goldberg and Gwyneth Paltrow. He had major roles in *No Looking Back*, *Row Your Boat*, *Vampires: Los Muertos*, *Little City*, *The Leading Man*, and *Homegrown*, among others. He appeared in the successful mainstream films *Pay It Forward* and *U-571*. He made a memorable guest television appearance on *Ally McBeal* and was written in for a short story line. Sarah Jessica Parker and fans of the HBO show *Sex and the City* remember Bon Jovi as Seth, the sexy Twister player who could not commit to women. In recent years Bon Jovi has not done as much acting and has seemed more focused on his music career. One of his only recent films was 2012's *New Year's Eve*, which did not do well at the box office or with the critics.

Jon Bon Jovi does get around. A unique opportunity to present himself as more than a rocker came in the form of an invitation to give the commencement address at Monmouth University, near West Long Branch, New Jersey. He gave the speech and received an honorary doctorate from the university on May 16, 2001. (Jon is not the only member of Bon Jovi to have received an honorary doctorate; in 2004, Richie Sambora received one from Kean University, a school he attended for one year.)

A commencement speaker has to satisfy the student body on graduation day. It does not matter who he knows on the board, how much money he has given, or what influence he garners in the outside world;

he has to deliver a spot-on address to win the student audience. Celebrities are often invited to give the commencement address at an academic institution. Most often they are alumni of the institution at which they are speaking (Matthew Fox, Columbia University; Alec Baldwin, New York University). This criterion does not apply to Jon Bon Jovi. With typical chutzpah, he did not let the fact that he did not have a college education deter him.

Jon Bon Jovi gave a heartfelt and honest speech focused on the graduating class. It would have been very easy to tell stories about his rock star life, but he made a point to make it meaningful to the students and parents. He hit all the right notes: passion, perseverance, gratefulness, and hopefulness. His own brand of determination was the main theme: "Right at this very moment, all across the country, thousands of graduates are receiving diplomas, some from schools like Yale, Georgetown and Dartmouth, who maybe think their piece of paper is more valuable (or their commencement speaker more impressive). Remember, we're from Jersey. We've been the underdogs all of our lives. And I can tell you this: it's passion, not pedigree, that can and will win in the end. Free yourself from comparison. Just because someone has fancy sneakers doesn't mean they can run faster."[13]

Jon's love and appreciation of competitive sports led him to a commercial opportunity in arena football. He had found an outlet where sports, philanthropy, and rock star glamour intersected. The aptly named Philadelphia Soul is a team based in Philadelphia, Pennsylvania. The team was started in 2004, and Jon Bon Jovi was one of the principal owners, along with band mate Richie Sambora as a minority owner. The team had great success, winning a couple of Arena Bowls and maintaining a reputation for having decent guys on the team. Not only did the players toss the ball on the field, but they also appeared in a Bon Jovi video to support the Soul Foundation. These were players that children could look up to as role models. Even the cheerleaders were above average. They had their own numbers and names on their jerseys and were included in team outreach activities equally with the players.

The tie-in of the Philadelphia Soul with Jon's Soul Foundation, paired with the concept of Philadelphia soul music, made up a potent cocktail of commercial opportunity. If you attended one of the Soul's games, you would no doubt have been informed about and asked for a donation to the Soul Foundation and heard some Bon Jovi music as well. The poor citizens of Philly never knew what hit them.

As anyone knows from watching *When We Were Beautiful*, Jon Bon Jovi is very interested in ownership of an NFL football team. For a wealthy sports enthusiast, NFL ownership guarantees a certain prestige and big money. Perhaps the Philadelphia Soul was a mere opening act to give him credibility in the industry. Only the future will tell; however, when the Arena Football League re-upped in 2011, Jon Bon Jovi was no longer an owner of the Soul.

Richie Sambora

Richie Sambora is used to having his personal problems in the news regularly. In a way, his problems have served as an impetus for keeping Bon Jovi's name in the press. Hopefully, Sambora's days of being an unintentional commercial for the band are over.

His very high-profile marriage to actress Heather Locklear is one of the main reasons for his press exposure. As a television actress Locklear was one of the most popular celebrities in the world in the '80s and '90s, with credits that included *Dynasty*, *Spin City*, *T.J. Hooker*, and *Melrose Place*. She has a history of dating famous men like Tom Cruise and Scott Baio, and in 1981 she married Tommy Lee of Mötley Crüe. Mötley Crüe and Bon Jovi were thrown together quite often in the '80s, since Doc McGhee managed both bands. Doc McGhee had a huge influence on the rock scene of the '80s; two of the biggest rock bands of that decade, Mötley Crüe and Bon Jovi, were under his management.

After a glamorous start to the marriage with a Paris wedding in 1994, the couple settled down to married life in California, and eventually had a daughter. Their divorce was finalized in 2007. Unfortunately, the end of the marriage unraveled with a misguided love triangle that included Locklear's former friend Denise Richards. Richards's marriage to bad boy Charlie Sheen helped to keep the ugly mess in the press. For a few weeks in 2011, Charlie Sheen (Carlos Estevez) was the most well-known celebrity in the world, as his bizarre, drug-fueled behavior kept him in the forefront of the media. His blatant disregard for any kind of decency was on display for all to see.

In the American celebrity world of six degrees of separation, Charlie Sheen was connected to Richie Sambora and was mentioned in many news stories about his international meltdown (Sheen was married to Richards. Richards occasionally dates Sambora. Sambora is divorced from the television actress Heather Locklear. Locklear and Richards used to be friends).

It used to be that Hollywood scandals could be contained in some way. Now that everyone's phone is a camera and a video recorder, that is not possible. YouTube clips are played millions of times a day, print media is archived on the Internet, and it is remarkably easy to forward salacious stories to friends. In the age of modern technology people are continually connected in ways they could never have imagined.

It has been reported in the press that both Richie Sambora and Heather Locklear have struggled with substance abuse problems over the years. While Sambora was quite open about his addictions in the only band-sanctioned Bon Jovi documentary, *When We Were Beautiful*, Locklear has not found an opportunity to do the same. Each of Sambora's DUI arrests and stints in rehabilitation has been mentioned by most of the major news outlets. Locklear's arrests for DUI and hit-and-run have also been reported. There have been reports in the news that Locklear has sought treatment for anxiety and depression. While she has not publicly acknowledged a problem or a visit to rehab, in early 2012 Reuters reported that she had been admitted to the hospital for treatment. The reason was a bad mix of alcohol and prescription drugs. Only husband and wife know the role that drugs and alcohol played in the demise of the Sambora marriage. The exposure of their problems in the media is a by-product of modern times. The fact is that people love to read about and watch other people's problems. As a country, America can't get enough of it. Our morbid curiosity about celebrities has only been enhanced and expanded by reality television and easy Internet access to junk news. One of the reasons may be that it is easier to focus on other people's problems than one's own. The fact that these two highly visible celebrities were together only increased their exposure. Despite the fact that the Samboras struggled with addiction, they did not let themselves act out their transgressions completely in the public eye; in fact, it probably came as a surprise to many when Richie Sambora left The Circle Tour to go to rehab. A rock musician in a rehabilitation program is akin to a fish in water. Steven Tyler (Aerosmith) is one example of a rock musician who has successfully completed rehab (after many years of struggle) and gained sobriety. He has reinvented his colored career in all the requisite ways: autobiography, Oprah interview, and television job (judge on *American Idol*). The list of musicians who have gone to rehab is long; the list of those who have reinvented themselves is much shorter. When musicians do get healthy, it is astonishing to note how Americans welcome them back. A person's attachment to music and the music artist is often impermeable.

Richie Sambora has long been respected as an accomplished rock guitarist. A talented songwriter, as well as singer, he has published three albums as solo projects. The first album, *Stranger in This Town*, was released in 1991; the second, *Undiscovered Soul*, in 1998. Neither album reached the top thirty on the United States charts, but they did better in Europe. A third album, *Aftermath of the Lowdown*, was released by Dangerbird Records in 2012.

In 2010, Richie Sambora pursued a commercial opportunity that may have surprised some: clothing design. Sambora and his partner, designer Nikki Lund, call their clothing line White Trash Beautiful. Sambora has strong ideas about how women should dress: "I like women in tight jeans, tight Capri pants or short skirts with great stockings."[14] Nikki Lund offers a more professional perspective: "The clothes are sophisticated and strong, sexy woman—for the *femme fatale*. I believe every single woman has a little bit of white trash in them and that every single woman wants to be sexy, and these clothes are designed to let a little bit of that diva out."[15] The line's debut was fairly well received in the fashion world and mainly consists of custom pieces. These clothes are not off the rack and available at the mall. Sambora has displayed his personal investment in the fashion enterprise by featuring his daughter, Ava, as one of the runway models; mom, Heather Locklear, sat in the audience, cheering her on and recording the event on her white iPhone.

David Bryan

David Bryan plays keyboards in Bon Jovi. Over the years, he has not been a part of the principal songwriting team with Jon and Richie, but he may have the last laugh as the most accomplished composer in the group. He has received, arguably, the most distinguished honor for songwriting of the band. In 2010, he was awarded the Tony Award for Best Musical, *Memphis*, from the American Theatre Wing. His partner on this project, Joe DiPietro, wrote the original story to accompany Bryan's original score. The score is jubilant and fun, and homage is paid to the rock and roll genre admirably. After a long incubation period in workshop, it finally made its way to Broadway in 2010. While most certainly a passion project for Bryan, *Memphis* is turning out to be a lucrative project for him as well. Its success in New York guarantees that communities and schools will want to perform it locally, and that means permissions and fees. There is also the requisite cast recording and merchandise available for sale. The prestige of winning the Tony Award has secured opportunities for Bryan to write another musical.

The seemingly overnight success of *Memphis* was the denouement of ten years of hard work composing music by Bryan. *Memphis* was not David Bryan's first musical; in 1999, he published *Sweet Valley High*, also with Joe DiPietro. His most recent collaboration with DiPietro is a musical titled *Chasing the Song*. Bryan has also composed music for films, such as 1990's *Netherworld*. In 2000, he released a solo instrumental album titled *Lunar Eclipse*.

Tico Torres

Tico Torres is considered the elder statesman of the band and is one of the most financially successful drummers in the world. His addiction issues have not been featured in the press like Richie Sambora's, and he has escaped much of the public scrutiny that goes along with that. On his third marriage and finally settled down, he has found commercial opportunities that interest him personally. In 2011, he started a clothing line for babies and children called Rock Star Baby. Featuring black and white as its signature colors, the collection includes a romper with a skull and crossbones on the front, little T-shirts that say things like "Rock Baby," tiny black sunglasses, cups and saucers, and so on. The collection is carried by Harrods in Europe, and one can also find the products online.

Torres is also a prolific artist. He has said that art gave him a chance to be spiritual about himself. His work has been displayed in gallery art shows and is sometimes available for sale. He has also donated his pictures for charity events.

Individually and collectively, the men of Bon Jovi have intelligently transformed themselves from an '80s "hair band" to commercially viable entities in several industries.

6

THE GENDER DIVIDE?

A band cannot be as successful and popular as Bon Jovi without appealing to both men and women. Having two of the top-grossing music tours since 2000 would suggest this, yet there is still a general presumption that Bon Jovi's music appeals to women more than men.

GENDER IN MUSIC ADVERTISING

When it comes to selling music, the gender of a performing artist is the foundation of the marketing plan; in addition, how a musical artist is perceived by his own and opposite gender is at the heart of building a fan base. For example, decades after she first began making hits, Madonna is still known as the musical artist who knows how to reinvent herself. This reinvention largely has to do with looks and appearance. In her early days, full net skirts, leggings, black rubber bracelets, scarves in her hair, and crazy big earrings made women notice her style. Later she used tight leather, harsh makeup, and stiletto heels to project another type of image, one that men would notice. These changes may have come from an artistic place, but they were definitely visually constructed to evoke a certain response from men and women.

Musical artists and their labels spend a significant amount of time and money to formulate, construct, and execute an image that teaches the public how to perceive them. They show the public what they want them to see. In some cases, the image of an artist can outweigh the artist's talent. It certainly seems likely that some artists' music comes as an afterthought to their marketability and sex appeal. For example, Britney Spears is not going to sing at Carnegie Hall any time soon, but she is referred to in the business as a great performer. Her career trajectory began with an overtly sexual music video that was built around the male schoolgirl fantasy. The purpose was to appeal to a male audience, as evidenced in her first video, "Hit Me Baby One More Time." The visual image of the school uniform with a ridiculously short skirt, thigh-high socks, push-up bra, open white shirt, and pigtails played on more than one male fantasy.

Bon Jovi has been clear about the intentions of executives and record companies to target female audiences in advertising the band. Keyboardist David Bryan has mentioned that "it didn't hurt that we were good looking."[1] Jon Bon Jovi has said many times that executives wanted to put his image in teen magazines in the '80s and sell him that way. Other musicians, like Bob Dylan and Bruce Springsteen, were not featured in those magazines, and Jon realized the importance of being taken seriously by the industry and his peers. He wanted to be on the cover of *Time* or *Rolling Stone* instead of *Teen Beat*. Eventually, the band learned to sell themselves in a manner they were comfortable with and took over their own management.

The term "sex appeal" is a little outdated, but that doesn't change the fact that it is an essential element for a rock band. In American music history there seems to be a strong correlation between gender and bands. In a wide generalization, but an accurate one, it seems that the more serious bands have a principally male audience, while the less serious bands have a predominantly female audience. This is not universally true, but it can be; for example, in the '80s, Metallica, Mötley Crüe, The Police, and Bruce Springsteen had predominantly male audiences. Duran Duran, Journey, Heart, and, yes, Bon Jovi drew more female fans. Another factor in this equation is the looks and personal appearance of the band members. In a recent survey at a series of Bon Jovi concerts, when asked why they liked Jon Bon Jovi as a performer, ninety-five percent of women polled said he was "hot," "cute," or "good looking." There are probably other reasons they like him, but they respond first to his looks.

Jon Bon Jovi is certainly aware of this reality. He goes out of his way to capitalize on it, but usually in a slightly subtle manner. He has appeared in print ads for Michael Kors wearing formal wear, and he is frequently photographed without his shirt when exercising or on vacation. Even with candid shots he is aware he is being photographed. In Bon Jovi music videos, Jon is featured to the exclusion of other band members. Everyone in the band knows who the most popular member is.

Jon's acting career has only reinforced his image as a quasi-lothario. He usually is cast as a bad boy (*Pay It Forward*, *Sex and the City*, *New Year's Eve*, *Little City*) or as someone who needs empathy (*Moonlight and Valentino*); both these character types appeal to women.

While he does it less these days, in the '80s and '90s, Jon would make a point to make some women feel special by actually bringing them up on stage for hugs, dancing, a slap on the rear, and even some kissing. The videos of this activity are available on YouTube. The women, of course, loved it. It was clearly innocent and in fun, but Jon knew that when he singled out one woman, all the rest would wish they were up there with him.

In concert, Jon has mentioned many times that he knows women expect him to "shake his rear." It almost seems like this expectation weighs heavily on his mind, and he wants to put it out there by speaking about it directly to the audience. While he seems to be kidding, it does come off as an uncomfortable admission from a man who wants to be admired for his music, not his rear end. One of his favorite moves on stage is to lift up his shirt as if he is overheated and sometimes using it to wipe his brow. The idea, of course, is to make the audience scream when they see his naked stomach. It is truly unbelievable that women of a certain age would be moved by that sight, but there it is. Jon has mentioned that he is like "Viagra for women," and that the men in the audience are "going to get lucky tonight when they get home." These comments are meant to engage the audience, but the truth of it is, Jon is not shy about the fact that he knows women love him.

There are three other band members up on stage with Jon: Richie Sambora, Tico Torres, and David Bryan. Do they have sex appeal? There are fans who favor one of the guys over Jon, but these individuals are in the minority (based on the previously mentioned survey).

Bon Jovi's particular brand of hard rock has always appealed to women (whether or not their music is really hard rock is a separate issue for discussion). Starting with the album *Bon Jovi* in 1984, women have always paid attention to this band. The reasons that women have been attracted to the band most likely include the fact that Jon Bon Jovi is the lead singer, their lyrics are not degrading toward women (on the whole), their music is entertaining, and they put on a great concert. During an interview on Redbeard's *In the Studio*, Jon Bon Jovi was asked if the album *Slippery When Wet* changed the rock and roll business. He responded:

> At that time, you know, I remember seeing somebody say "they made hard rock accessible to women, and to the masses." And there's validity in that statement. It was Dee Snider who I saw say that . . . and he's right because all of a sudden, the guys who were going to see AC/DC and those guys, or ZZ, you know, or Scorpions and those kinds of bands . . . suddenly, they saw me on TV twenty years ago sing "you give love a bad name" to a girl, and bang zoom the poster industry's got a big spike. It was a lot of influence in girls' bedrooms . . . there were pictures of us.[2]

It is telling that as Jon Bon Jovi is discussing his music's influence he quickly relates it to publicity posters in "girls' bedrooms." Jon himself seems unsure what won over fans: Jon Bon Jovi's sex appeal or the influence of the band's music. It is most likely a combination of both. Jon is acutely aware of the fact that his looks are an integral part of the band's long success, and there is no denying that the handsomeness of the lead singer can make or break a band. It can also have a great deal of influence on how a band's music is interpreted. For example, in the heavy metal genre it is not unusual for male fans to gravitate toward a lead singer who is less pretty boy and more real or rugged: James Hetfield of Metallica or Dee Snider of Twisted Sister, for example. On the other hand, within the hard rock genre, women may gravitate more toward Bret Michaels of Poison or Jon Bon Jovi.

As discussed in chapter three, MTV had a huge effect on the selling of Bon Jovi in the '80s. The revolutionary music television channel allowed viewers to see their favorite artists up close and personal and in live performance. If they had never had the opportunity to attend a concert, all they had to do was turn on their television (now they can turn on their television, desktop, laptop, iPad, tablet, or cell phone). One of the inevitable outcomes of the MTV revolution was that viewers did not solely judge music on what they were hearing, but also on what they were seeing. In Bon Jovi's case, the visual of the band probably drew the interest of women before the music did. Because women saw Bon Jovi on MTV, they wanted to listen to their music. Because they liked Bon Jovi's music, the men were more attractive.

In the '80s and '90s, album covers had important relevance to a band's career. The album cover was a piece of art and an expression of what the band or artist wanted to communicate to the buyer about the content of the record. The buying of a record was often the first time a fan saw the band that made the music he loved. Fans were not inundated with images of them on the Internet. Purchasing a record was a ritual that took place in a store, not online, and involved a sense of the aesthetic in a way it just doesn't today. Choosing the record; unwrapping it with anticipation, not knowing exactly what you would find; seeing the pictures of your favorite artist as a surprise, because they had not been previously published; and reading the text inside the cover were all part of the magic of buying an album. The appeal of the album cover to fans would make or break the sale.

There are some album covers in music history that have achieved iconic status; Pink Floyd's *Dark Side of the Moon* is an example. The angular multicolored image will be forever associated with the band. Even someone who has never listened to their music may associate Pink Floyd with that album cover. Bruce Springsteen's *Born in the U.S.A.* is another example. The cover does not show his face, but the average person on the street who is shown that picture would most likely know it was a Bruce Springsteen album. The red cap in the back pocket of his faded jeans and the use of red, white, and blue convey the heart of the album immediately upon a glance.

Bon Jovi is no different from other bands in that they need to feel comfortable that the cover image conveys the content of the record as intended. Their most well-known album, *Slippery When Wet*, is an example of how vital an album cover is to the sales of a record. The original concept for *Slippery* was a picture of a woman in a shower stall, with the words "Slippery When Wet" written on the steamy shower door. Unfortunately, this is not an untypical concept for a rock band. The genre often features images of scantily clad—and sometimes denigrated—women on its album covers; examples include Ted Nugent's *Love Grenade*, Whitesnake's *LoveHunter*, Guns N' Roses' *Appetite for Destruction*, and the Scorpions' *Virgin Killer*.

When Jon Bon Jovi saw a mock-up of the cover of *Slippery* proposed by the record company, he was not pleased. Instead of a woman in a shower stall, all that was visible was a woman's torso clad in a T-shirt with a hot pink background (the art director chose that color because it matched the model's fingernail polish). Jon Bon Jovi remembers: "The album cover was hot pink, and we as a rock and roll community had just witnessed what hot pink did to a certain artist during a video and I'll never forget who that artist was. . . . I thought *pink, pink*, why *pink*?"[3]

There is no way to verify which artist Jon is referencing without asking him directly; however, it is most likely that he is talking about the unfortunate Billy Squier, whose 1984 video "Rock Me Tonite" ruined his career. In the mid-1980s, Squier was enjoying a healthy career and performing to packed venues when the Kenny Ortega–directed "Rock Me Tonite" video was released. Squier has said that the backlash and the reaction to the video were immediate. As soon as the video was released, he saw his audience diminishing with each show of the tour. Watching the video will explain why the audiences left. There has never really been anything exactly like it. There are cream-colored satin sheets, a pink tank top, and the kind of dancing we all do when we are alone and think we look good. Men who had liked Squier's music did not want to be associated with him after the video came out. It may have been homophobia, or simply a case of realizing the man and his music were not what they seemed. For whatever reason, Squier's label, Capitol Records, should have done something to protect his career. The real shame of it is that the song was really good.

Because of what they witnessed happen to Billy Squier, Bon Jovi could not and would not reconcile the color hot pink with what they were trying to accomplish artistically. Jon spoke to the CEO/president of the record label and the art director. Jon spoke plainly to the CEO: "This will be the demise of the band. You like the record, we like the record. Please don't do this."[4] Jon was told that production had started and that the single was released, so they could not delay, but the CEO gave Jon a few hours to put together a new cover. Jon and photographer Mark Weiss got together and came up with a new idea: "And I went to the same photographer . . . and I shot a garbage bag with a squirt bottle of water. But it looked like the galaxy, it looked like stars, and so I said to him 'wait, wait, wait, shoot it again with the water and I wrote with my fingers . . . 'Slippery When Wet' and I said 'there's your album cover. . . .' I said 'remember *Back in Black*? Here's your album cover. Forget it. Just turn it in.'"[5] Jon had said that the music was more important than art to him. He wanted the album to positively reflect the artistic intent of the band. It was fortunate that he had the chance to reimage the album cover so it aligned with his own vision, as many artists do not have the opportunity to negotiate with the record label about how their albums are marketed.

In a radio interview, Jon was asked if any of the original *Slippery* covers were produced and sold before the cover was changed. He responded: "They're very, very, very rare. They were strictly the first run of the Japanese import . . . but in those days you know Japan had a longer lead-time. It squeaked out over there . . . but that was the only place."[6]

The *Slippery* album would turn out to be one of the biggest albums of the '80s, and Bon Jovi's biggest album ever. The original album cover would have most certainly attracted a male audience, but would have most likely repelled a female one (a close-up of a woman's breasts in a wet T-shirt would have sent a strong message about women, and certainly not a pro-feminist one). The black garbage bag cover was a choice made because Jon Bon Jovi did not like the color pink associated with the band's name. It is interesting to consider how the other cover would have affected album sales to women and, consequently, the building of the band's female fan base.

THE BON JOVI AUDIENCE

Jon Bon Jovi's good looks, charm, and general appeal first drew Bon Jovi's female audience. Not to be completely outdone, Richie, David, Tico, and Alec all had individual appealing personalities that attracted women as well. The band's fun, memorable tunes and universal lyrics appealed to men and women, and their singular music videos drew teen audiences of both sexes in the mid-1980s. It has been mentioned that Bon Jovi was one of the first hard rock or metal bands that really appealed to women, and women did embrace the band from the beginning. Certainly there were female fans that liked Jon Bon Jovi from videos and fan magazines first and the music second, but there were also female fans who liked the music first and the man second. While it has been suggested by some music critics and industry people that Bon Jovi is a "girl" heavy metal band, there is no doubt that men have enjoyed their music as well.

New Jersey native Ed Jankowski recalls that his male friends liked Bon Jovi in the '80s: "Guys liked Bon Jovi. People from New Jersey are very proud of the state. Bon Jovi made it big and were from New Jersey. I went to one concert in high school at Giants Stadium and the audience was 60/40 female/male."[7] Jankowski shared that his other favorite bands in high school, in the '80s, were Def Leppard, Poison, Van Halen, and Warrant. He attended a Van Halen concert in Washington, D.C., in 2012 and estimated the audience to be ninety percent male.[8] Van Halen and Bon Jovi are two bands that were huge in the '80s and are still performing today. One is more likely to see more women than men at a Bon Jovi concert today, while the opposite is true for Van Halen. Why? Information taken from a poll at Bon Jovi concerts in 2008 and 2010 on the U.S. East Coast reveals that the most common reason is that women "like" Jon Bon Jovi. They reveal reasons like: "he is cute," "he is a family man," and "he is a good person." Further discussion reveals that people like the music and the fact that the band has been around a long time. It seems that women must genuinely like the lead singer of a band to become a fan.

Since the beginning of rock and roll history, the lead singer of a band has been the key to success. It is interesting to consider how looks and appearance influence music and vice versa. If Elvis had looked like Bob Dylan, but sounded the exact same and sang all his own songs, would he have won a female audience? Would his music have been as popular? When considering Bon Jovi's contemporary Poison, is it possible to imagine the band having any commercial success without Bret Michaels as their lead singer? The band Van Halen has historically been much better received by critics than Bon Jovi, but the band has not won as many female fans. One possible reason may be that women could not, and did not, identify with David Lee Roth, and later Sammy Hagar, as lead singer. There is nothing wrong with their performing styles or personas, but ultimately some women do not find them appealing. It seems that cute men can sell rock and roll to women better than less-cute men. Bret Michaels, Elvis, and Jon Bon Jovi are cases in point.

Jon is well aware that his appearance matters very much in his profession. Even today, thirty years into his career, he works hard to look good. When he gains ten pounds he "feels fat." He exercises manically while acting like it is no big deal, and is careful about what he eats. While he claims he has not had any plastic surgery, he definitely does more to keep up his looks than the average fifty-year-old man. He continues to suffer the fact that journalists write about his looks. Tom Gliatto of *People*: "After all, the body is still lean and muscular—he runs daily and hits the weights up to five times a week—and the hair is blond and full, if less elaborately highlighted and blow-dried than when Bon Jovi the band was at its peak with albums like 1986's *Slippery When Wet*."[9] Even *Men's Health* has something to say about the handsome Bon Jovi: "He had his looks—strong chin, brilliant smile, gorgeous teeth, perfectly feathered hair. He had that butt, often commented upon but never in a gross way."[10] It is hard to imagine a journalist writing about Bruce Springsteen or Bono this way. In performance, Jon's wardrobe is carefully chosen to emphasize certain assets. Everything is tight fitting, and what is not tight is usually left open (button-up shirt). He carefully selects what he wears to seduce his audience (women) and then spends two to three hours making it look like he does not care, like he did not put any thought into it. All in all, his image has been carefully cultivated over decades, by someone who knows the power of appearance after seeing himself in countless photographs and on film. Extreme self-awareness is certainly not a trait exclusive to Jon Bon Jovi. Professionals in film, television, sports, music, and politics are hyper-aware of the power an image can have on a career, whether it be positive or negative.

In 2006, the *New York Times* made an important point about Bon Jovi's staying power and how that longevity affected the fan base: "There is one sure way to sustain an arena-size rock career past the two-decade mark: Stay exactly the same. And like his fellow Jersey boy Bruce Springsteen, Bon Jovi has done just that. At 44 he has the same boyish face, hard-rock sound, working-class values and dramatic hair as he did in his 20s. There is something comforting about his undying relevance, as if as long as he is advising fans to 'hold on to what we've got,' there will always be small-town men who marry their high school sweethearts, sell 100 million records and live in chateaus in unfairly maligned states."[11]

Women and Bon Jovi

Jon Bon Jovi's long-term marriage is a crucial and integral component of his success. Women fans like the fact that he is married. He has benefitted from the stability and comfort of a loyal wife and close-knit family since he married Dorothea Hurley in 1989. The couple's history is like a fairy tale with an adult twist. The fairy-tale part is that they sat next to each other in high school classes, were married on the spur of the moment, were blessed with four children, and have stayed married for the majority of their adult lives. The adult twist is that they took a crucial break from each other in their mid-twenties, when Bon Jovi was in the flush of fame, and that Jon Bon Jovi is a very famous rock star.

The Bon Jovis' marriage is the exception, not the rule, for celebrity marriages. It probably helps that Dorothea is not famous herself and does not have a public career. Within their peer group it is challenging to come up with a list of people who have stayed married to their original partner as long as they have. Bono and Ali Hewson are perhaps the only ones.

What is notable about his marriage is that it has given Jon Bon Jovi a certain credibility with female (and male) audiences. He has been cited as an example of a "family man" in the mainstream press several times, and his marital status and wife are often inquired about and commented on in interviews: "I mean, family man, what a concept," he said not long ago, somewhat dazedly. "I mean, how'd I end up the poster boy for that?"[12]

A poll taken at Bon Jovi concerts in 2008 and 2010 asked concertgoers why they were fans of Jon Bon Jovi; the responses included "he's stayed married to the same woman," "he has good values," "he seems like a good guy." None of these public opinions would probably ring as true if Jon Bon Jovi were divorced, dating a younger celebrity or model, or having legal or substance abuse problems (like some of his contemporaries). The appeal of Jon Bon Jovi being married is twofold for female fans: he is safe to lust after because he is loyally married, and it seems easier to support and endorse a rock star who is stable and married than one who is not. Women respect him for staying with his first wife; it makes him special.

When Jon Bon Jovi is inevitably asked about his marriage in interviews, he has a few themes he sticks with, and the following is a good example: "It's hard work and determination. My wife of eighteen years, Dorothea, is really my best friend, and I wouldn't want to be with anybody else in the world. And I don't even wanna hang around anybody else. It's that simple. I got it right the first time." [13]

As a culture, America is obsessed with celebrity marriages and seems to have more interest in the demise of a marriage than its fairy-tale beginning. Celebrity marriages often make up the cover stories of popular magazines and are constant subject matter in the mainstream media. Americans care about who marries whom, what kind of ceremony they have, what they are wearing, and who attended the festivities. When the inevitable breakup is announced on the Internet, there is speculation on the details of the breakup: the how and why, and the arrangements spelled out in a prenuptial agreement. When the celebrity marries again, there is cause for remembering the first spouse and where it all went wrong, as well as speculation as to whether or not the next marriage will work.

Couples who are together at certain moments in their careers will always be together in the psyche of the general public. For example, Elvis was living with Ginger Alden when he died in 1973, but Priscilla Presley will always be his wife. Fleetwood Mac's sordid history is legendary in the music world, but Stevie Nicks and Lindsey Buckingham had a public and heartfelt romance for a long while. They broke up in the '80s, and he is now married with three children, but for Fleetwood Mac fans, the wife is a nonentity. When Stevie and Lindsey are on stage together it might as well be 1980. Paul McCartney has been through some tough times finding the right partner after he lost his wife of twenty-nine years to cancer. It doesn't matter that he is on his third marriage, or that Linda McCartney was married before she was with Paul. The images and legacy of Linda and Paul McCartney will prevail in the history books.

For Bon Jovi fans, Richie Sambora stands out as the band member with the big divorce because he was married to a very famous woman. Heather Locklear and Richie Sambora were much admired as a couple by fans and the general public. Most likely, fans of Sambora will studiously ignore his relationship with the much younger, and tabloid friendly, Denise Richards. Her marriage to Charlie Sheen, her reality television show, and her betrayal of former friend Heather Locklear cannot be erased from many fans' memories. She is the other woman. Tico

Torres was also married to someone famous. His second marriage, which ended in 1998, was to supermodel Eva Herzigová.

For all the previously mentioned reasons, Jon Bon Jovi is regarded favorably when it comes to how he conducts his personal life. In public, he will happily speak about how much he loves his wife, but it tends to be regurgitated rhetoric; he doesn't really reveal much. Dorothea does not reveal anything either. She is an intensely private person and fastidiously avoids public life. When asked by *People* magazine what it is like to be married to Jon, she replied: "I've literally had women crawl over me to get to the band. . . . I don't know if it's stupid enough or smart enough . . . to think he's going to come home to me at the end of the day. So I'm not going to sit and bite my nails and get gray hair over it." [14] Dorothea's attitude clearly shows that she is able to emotionally handle a lifestyle that must be extremely challenging at times. She has most likely seen some things over the years that no wife should have to witness. The fact that she has been able to stay married is a testament to her sense of self and level of patience. In the same *People* interview, Jon Bon Jovi is much more plainspoken than his wife: "Rock and roll is a business of excess—there is nothing I can't get two of," he says, getting heated in his own defense. "If I wanted two pizzas, I could get it. If I wanted two women, I could get it. But I don't need two pizzas. And I don't need two girls. And it would be nobody's business if I decided I wanted to eat both of those pizzas by myself anyhow." [15] Whatever goes on behind closed doors, it is to the Bon Jovis ' credit that they have managed to raise their children well and keep their personal life private as much as they have.

Interestingly, Jon Bon Jovi does not usually wear his wedding ring onstage when performing. The standard reason given is that the ring can clank against the microphone stand in performances and make noise. But it is possibly a strategy for helping his female fans think of him as a single man. When he first was married, this was also a concern for Bon Jovi's management: "Bon Jovi's management reportedly had hoped the wedding would stay secret, on the theory that single rock stars are sexier." [16]

Men and Bon Jovi

There is a misconception that men do not like Bon Jovi. If this were true, the band would not have sold over 130 million records. Men seem to like and respect Jon Bon Jovi as much as female fans. One man at a Bon Jovi concert in Washington, D.C., in 2010 described how the band kept him from total despair at a crucial time in his life. He remembers: "When my brother was murdered, Bon Jovi saved my life . . . they are my inspiration."[17] New Jerseyite Ed Jankowski has described how the boys at his high school respected and appreciated, and took great pride in, the fact that the band was from their home state.[18] Even the *New York Times* has weighed in on this issue, with Kevin Cahillane's article "Adolescent Angst: When the Karate Kid Fell for Jon Bon Jovi." Cahillane reveals the following: "Somewhere along the way, too, I got the impression that guys who listened to Bon Jovi best left that fact buried in the closet, next to those dog-eared copies of *Playboy*. But let's face it. I'm not cool. I drive a minivan."[19] Early music videos and concerts of the band clearly show many men in the audience. Men have attended, and will continue to attend, Bon Jovi concerts because they enjoy the music as much as the women do.

In American culture, there are certain traits or characteristics that can label a band for women or for men, yet overt femininity in a rock band does not repel men. Kiss is one example of a group of men not afraid to wear makeup, although it is clearly theatrical in nature, and Kiss has a predominantly male fan base. Mötley Crüe is considered a "man's band" because of their extreme heavy metal sound; however, they have worn makeup and heels in a clear nod to cross-dressing and have not had trouble cultivating a strong male audience.

HARDLY FEMINISTS

In 2010, just as Bon Jovi was cresting toward the peak of a record-breaking year of touring and promoting their *Circle* album, the band encountered an unfortunate reminder of the past. Photographs from an ill-advised photo session in the '80s were made public. The pictures were printed in a book by former Bon Jovi tour manager Rich Bozzett and were widely published on the Internet and various media outlets, including TMZ. The black-and-white pictures were apparently taken by rock photographer Ross Marino in 1985, during a publicity photo shoot. They feature all five members of Bon Jovi lying on a bed with several young, scantily clad women. The story is that, as former manager of the band, Bozzett pocketed negatives of the photo shoot and decided to release them in conjunction with the publication of his book. He has claimed that he is not retaliating against Bon Jovi or trying to make money from the pictures. The pictures are more ridiculous than any-thing else. The guys look like they are having a good time, and the women seem enamored, but the scene is clearly staged. If Bozzett's intention was to suggest that the pictures were anything but a tacky publicity concept, he hopelessly failed.

Overall, the pictures failed to make a permanent mark on Bon Jovi's career. The *New York Post* did run an article on it, questioning Jon Bon Jovi's family man status. The fans did not turn away. It turns out that Jon Bon Jovi had nothing to fear from the release of the pictures. According to fan forums on the Bon Jovi website, Bozzett's book was universally rejected and declared "trash." Amazingly, fans did not seem to care that the band put themselves in a precarious position, nor that the women were mostly naked while the men kept their clothes on; the pictures were not an issue. The consensus seems to be that the incident should stay in the past where it belongs. The exposed pictures were not a deal breaker for Bon Jovi fans.

The lyrics of a song give insight into the writer's perspective and attitude. It is up to the individual to interpret the meaning of a given lyric. Bon Jovi's lyrics are not misogynistic, but some of their earlier work displays immaturity. There are a few lyrics that cast women as less than whole. For example, these lyrics from "Social Disease": "So full of high grade octane she could run the bullet train on 38 double Ds." In "Runaway," Bon Jovi's first hit song, women are referred to as being made of "lipstick, plastic, and paint." "In and Out of Love" describes the role of the woman: "She's here to make my life complete and then I'm long gone I got another show." The band's more recent material seems to avoid lyrics that denigrate women.

Discounting the previous examples, women respond best to Bon Jovi lyrics that emphasize commitment. "In Your Arms," "Born to Be My Baby," and "I'll Be There for You" are a few examples. "I'll be there for you, these five words I swear are true" may seem simple enough, but they are not the type of lyrics you often hear in hard rock. For some reason the lyrics "you were born to be my baby and baby I was made to be your man" come across as heartfelt and sincere when Jon sings them. In performance, songs like these are usually the audience favorites after megahits "Livin' on a Prayer" and "Dead or Alive."

Compared to other musical acts in the American mainstream, Bon Jovi's offenses against women are minor. There has been much discussion in the mainstream media of the hip-hop (Nelly, Eminem) and heavy rock and metal (Kid Rock, Rob Zombie) musical genres and their often degrading lyrics toward women. The consequences and influence of these types of lyrics have been debated before Congress and brought to cultural awareness by organizations such as the National Research Center for Women and Families.

Throughout the Bon Jovi documentary *When We Were Beautiful*, it is made abundantly clear that Bon Jovi is a male-dominated planet. Women are welcome to visit, but are not invited to stay. "Girls" is the common word for anyone of the female gender. In the documentary, there is one revealing moment when Jon Bon Jovi, discussing touring, shares his opinion about the role of the rock star wife: "True, it isn't a democracy. There are bands that have five members and then five wives all have equal votes. The day that the bass player's wife tells me when I'm gonna tour? Ain't comin'. It's never comin'."[20] Whether this is an anti-feminist remark, or just a reminder that Jon Bon Jovi is the one in charge, it speaks to the place of women within the Bon Jovi operation. Bon Jovi never forgets it is women who keep the band in business.

7

THE BON JOVI BRAND

The branding of rock bands has reached a new level in the 21st century. The number of albums sold used to be the primary measure of success for rock bands. In today's climate, the quality and breadth of a band's brand is what determines success. Also, it is just not enough to sell music; entrepreneurship is expected of bands that have accumulated massive wealth. The money must be invested, cultivated, and repurposed in meaningful and profitable ways. Some of the biggest musical acts in recent history have focused on areas of finance, politics, and social media to hone their brands, and therefore increased their wealth.

Musician, author, and entrepreneur Jimmy Buffett is one example of an American artist who has taken music branding to the next level. His philosophy of party at the beach has made him a wealthy man. He has somehow taken his only top ten hit, "Margaritaville," and turned it into a yearly estimated income of over $40 million. Besides a nonfiction book that went straight to number one on the *New York Times* Best Seller list, there are "Margaritaville" restaurants, a resort, clothing stores, various merchandise, food stores, and a tequila business. He clearly has an astute business methodology in addition to musical talent. Buffett epitomizes what *Forbes* magazine describes as the "power of branding": "A brand is more than a name—it is the sum total of a consumer's experiences with a recognizable product—and it is powerful."[1] This power has been cultivated to great effect by other top-earning bands, including U2, Van Halen, Kiss, Aerosmith, the Rolling Stones, the Beatles, and Bon Jovi. Along with the power of a brand

comes opportunities to expand into multiple ventures, and these bands
have certainly taken advantage of them. If the members of these bands
got together they would more likely be discussing stock profits, the
economy, and investment opportunities than music.

Forbes magazine has classified the bands mentioned above into a
group known as "old rockers who have turned into top business people," and Jon Bon Jovi is no exception.[2] Since he took control of his own
management in the early '90s he has used his considerable skills as a
leader and entrepreneur to market his Bon Jovi brand all over the globe
with undeniably positive results (130 million albums sold, myriad
awards, loyal fan base). By starting with albums and touring and moving
outward to philanthropy, professional sports, merchandising, politics,
and various business ventures, Bon Jovi has moved beyond rock band
status and has permeated everyday American culture. The Bon Jovi
brand has been visible in professional sports (the Philadelphia Soul,
NFL performances), at the Tony Awards (David Bryan's *Memphis*), in
tabloid media (Richie Sambora and Denise Richards), in philanthropy
(Soul Foundation, Soul Kitchen), in film (documentary *When We Were
Beautiful*), in Jon Bon Jovi's individual films and television shows (*U-
571*, *Pay It Forward*, *Sex and the City*, *Ally McBeal*), on television
(Grammy Awards, NBC, Bravo, CMT), in commercials (Advil), in social
media news (Steve Jobs vs. Jon Bon Jovi, the death hoax), and even in
politics (the White House Council for Community Solutions). While
this is not a comprehensive list by any means, it is clear that Bon Jovi
have woven themselves into the tapestry of American daily life in a way
no one could have predicted. It is difficult to name an American band
that has equaled them in reaching as many venues in American culture.
It really is a Bon Jovi world.

The core of Bon Jovi's brand has always been hardworking guys from
New Jersey. The brand image they have projected over the years has
undergone a metamorphosis, but they have always been more T-shirts
and jeans than designer. They have worked very hard to maintain this
image despite their great wealth. Jon Bon Jovi has described how, in the
earlier days, the record labels wanted to market them as a "cute band"
but they preferred casual T-shirts and jeans.[3] The concept of the New
Jersey work ethic has been accepted as universally true by fans (of
course it doesn't hurt that Bruce Springsteen was taking his New Jersey
work ethic on the road before Bon Jovi was out of high school, laying

the foundation upon which they could build). In interviews and the press, the band often speaks of staying true to their roots, never forgetting where they came from, and working hard. These sound bites have been repeated over and over again, and the values expressed in them have become synonymous with the band.

THE DISCOGRAPHY AS BRAND

The music of a band is the core of any music marketing campaign. How a musical act is visually presented is also of key importance; therefore, the music and the album cover art together make up the brand of any band (an example of brand confusion would be Bruce Springsteen photographed on an album cover wearing a tuxedo, or Lady Gaga making public appearances in jeans). Bon Jovi have had many looks throughout their career and, in their fifties, seem to be settled into an age-appropriate look that works for them. They have learned that brand recognition must be logical. Musical acts that understand themselves, know what they want to present to the public, and are clear in their musical intentions know how to market themselves. Bon Jovi is no exception.

From the first album, released in 1984, to the present, there has been a consistency in the marketing and branding of Bon Jovi's music. The overall musical style of the band is one of traditional rock, sometimes more heavy (*Keep the Faith*, *In and Out of Love*), sometimes more light (*You Don't Know Me*, *Bed of Roses*), and sometimes a little bit country (*Lost Highway*, *Who Says You Can't Go Home*), but the music has always been marketed as no-nonsense American rock.

A key aspect of the way the music is marketed is the central focus on Jon Bon Jovi. He is usually featured in some way on the album cover. On the debut album he was photographed alone in the street, with the rest of the band on the back cover. The second album, *7800° Fahrenheit*, featured his face framed by fire. On *Cross Road* and *Crush* his face loomed largest of the guys on the cover. Other album covers have ranged from images of an open highway with a view from the dashboard (*Lost Highway*) to a large array of satellite dishes (*Bounce*) to images of the band in shadow (*The Circle*). On the whole, the covers of Bon Jovi's

albums have supported the idea of brotherhood, with Jon predominantly featured.

For the most part Bon Jovi's prolific discography has had a positive
effect on their brand name. Even their least successful records sell well
somewhere on the globe, if not in the United States (their first gold
record was in Japan). How a band looks and what they wear is almost as
vital as the music. How the market perceives a band is crucial to its
success.

Over the band's career, Bon Jovi has seen the universal standard for
music production, the album, become for all intents and purposes a
historical fact; it is no longer the standard for delivering music to audiences. Digital music is here to stay and will ultimately replace the physical album/compact disc as we know it. The proof is the fact that 1.27
billion individual tracks were digitally downloaded in the United States
in 2011.[4] It makes sense that in the time of endless choice (coffee at
Starbucks, social media, Amazon) people expect the same when selecting their music. The drive for and expectation of immediate gratifica-
tion combined with short attention spans has greatly shifted people's
perceived value in purchasing an entire album. During the first decade
of the 21st century, album revenues fell approximately eight percent
each year.[5]

MARKETING A BRAND

The Bon Jovi brand has been built using both standard and innovative
methods. The standard methods include publishing albums, performing, and touring. The innovative methods involve touring internationally
before it was commonplace, being at the top of the digital music trend,
packaging, and targeted marketing. Mixed media packaging is not an
innovative idea in itself (Prince utilized it on his 2005 Musicology Tour,
for example), but Bon Jovi has capitalized on it. They produced an all-in
presale for their 2008 Lost Highway Tour, which bundled a ticket and
digital album sold as one transaction via Ticketmaster. Another example
of bundled marketing was utilized on the Have a Nice Day Tour in
2005. A concert on this tour was the first live full-length concert
streamed on Sprint wireless. Sprint was a sponsor of the tour and made
it possible for fans to view a live Bon Jovi show on their cell phones. In

2010 the band offered live streaming the first thirty minutes of their Munich concert via Ustream.

The band has also utilized various merchandise bundles to promote albums. The Bon Jovi merchandise does include something for everyone. There is even a "Jon Bon Jovi for President" button. Despite all the commercial endeavors of the band, Jon Bon Jovi insists that the merchandise and upselling is not the point: "The commerce is really just a by-product of the art."[6] It is certainly easier to disregard millions in annual merchandise sales when you are extremely wealthy than when you are a struggling young artist who cannot get a record deal. Jon Bon Jovi's stage name is all over not only the Bon Jovi merchandise but also his Soul Foundation merchandise. With an estimated $2 million per year in merchandising sales, it would seem there are many people proudly wearing Jon's name.

The Backstage with Bon Jovi fan club offers promotions intended to entice people to buy tickets, but it also strives to make concerts events that involve travel, fan club get-togethers, and assorted auxiliary events. Their website mentions "sharing the event with other Bon Jovi fans."[7] Bon Jovi is not just selling tickets; they are community building among their fans. There are plenty of active discussion forums on the Backstage site where fans share all kinds of information about the band. Each fan profile includes details on how long the individual has been a member of BSBJ (Backstage Bon Jovi). When the band is touring, fans plan meet-ups and different events around the concert itself.

It is a phenomenon of Bon Jovi's culture, and other bands', that fans enjoy the aspect of community. They communicate on band forums, create fan websites, and share stories about their lives and Bon Jovi's place in them. They meet each other at concerts and surrounding events and stay in touch. This type of community environment is clearly an offshoot of modern social media, and has definitely taken hold. There is an immediate level of trust among the fans, a comfort level, and a joint purpose: to love Bon Jovi.

It is difficult to determine whether Bon Jovi's marketing spurred the need for "VIP events" or the Bon Jovi community developed out of attending these events. Either way, the VIP events are increasingly popular at Bon Jovi concerts, and with other musical acts. Like just about everything else, music has created a top-level experience for those fans for whom buying tickets just isn't enough. A typical VIP package would most likely include premium seating for the concert, a dinner or reception before the concert, a backstage—and possibly on-stage—tour, and merchandise including T-shirts, sweatshirts, tote bags, etc. The epitome of the VIP experience is a meet-and-greet opportunity to meet the band and have a photo made, and at some venues there is special parking provided. There is usually a special check-in desk at will call and staff on hand to handle the VIPs. (Bon Jovi does not typically offer the meet and greet as part of their VIP package. They don't need to; fans buy the tickets anyway.) At the lower end, the average ticket price for an experience like this can start somewhere around $1,200. It makes sense to question why someone would pay so much for a back-stage experience that does not include meeting the band. It may be that the proximity to the rock and roll lifestyle is enough to satisfy the seri-ous fan. It could also be that prime seating is a priority for a small percentage of fans, who will pay anything for a close enough look.

Bon Jovi's success has been largely due to the fact that demographi-cally they have a wide audience. In the early '80s the demographic seemed to be mostly teens. This makes sense, since they were a new band and teens watched MTV in the '80s. However, over the thirty years the band has been active, that demographic has expanded to include audiences of several generations (Baby Boomer, Generation X, Generation Y, younger teens, children of original fans), genres of music (country), and continents (North America, Asia).

As the band became aware of the expansion of the fan base, they responded with clear intentions to win new fans. They embraced the change, and, as a result, the change worked to their advantage. The 2000 video "It's My Life" is a clear example of the band marketing to a younger teen audience. The slickly produced video features a story line about two teens, with the band functioning as a kind of Greek chorus. The marketing of the song and video achieved the impossible by mak-ing the band appear fresh. The popularity of *Crush* and the hit single drew the attention of younger audiences and hooked a new fan base. Bon Jovi later did the same thing when they recorded *Lost Highway* in Nashville and performed a hugely popular duet, "Who Says You Can't Go Home" with country star Jennifer Nettles. The album drew the attention of country music fans and pleased existing fans as well. Again, the band achieved the impossible by seamlessly transitioning success-fully to country music and then returning to their rock and roll roots with no fallout. This bold move drew the attention of the music industry and fans alike. It is difficult to know whether Bon Jovi anticipated the attention they received for trying something different with the *Lost Highway* album. The event was a noticeable one that year in American music.

There are teens and younger children today who are fans of Bon Jovi. How did this happen? One reason may be that the original Bon Jovi fan base has had children and includes them in their Bon Jovi worship. This includes listening to their music together, and bringing multiple generations of families to concerts. Mothers and daughters together at a Bon Jovi concert is a common sight. The marketing of the band's merchandise reflects an awareness of this fact. The Bon Jovi clothing line comes in children's sizes. Jon Bon Jovi has commented that he "knows there are two generations of fans out there" and that he's "known that for the last decade."[8] As a result, the organization will most likely continue to court younger fans and make the Bon Jovi concert a family-friendly environment. As a result, there is notably much less onstage flirting by Jon today than there was in the late 1990s and early 2000s.

Jon's father, the senior Bongiovi, has marketed the Bongiovi brand as well, with a line of pasta sauces. He has announced a line of tomato sauces that reflect the family's Sicilian traditions in the kitchen. They are available online in a variety of flavors.

Another unexpected marketing opportunity occurred in 2012. Surprisingly, Jon Bon Jovi entered into a partnership with Avon Products, Inc., to market two new Avon fragrances known as "Unplugged." Jon will appear in "Him" and "Her" ads to market the perfume. He commented on the business relationship: "Avon, and the Avon Foundation for Women, have given support and a voice to those in need for decades; their philosophy of empowerment sends a strong message and I'm pleased to partner with them."[9] The business move was most likely a wise one for Jon. The Avon brand caters to middle-aged women who will love to wear Jon Bon Jovi every day.

A GLOBAL BRAND

When it comes to distributing their records on an international scale, Bon Jovi is ahead of the curve. Jon Bon Jovi understood early in his career, possibly from the massive audience response on tours of Japan, that cultivating multiple markets was one way to ensure financial stability. Jon has said that the band never had to depend on one market to distribute their records.[10] This approach has clearly had a positive effect on their longevity and taking the band's brand to a global marketplace. For example, in certain countries one would not expect, like in Australia, Bon Jovi is extremely popular. A 2010 concert in Abu Dhabi drew the largest crowd ever at that venue. Having a prominent fan base in various countries has taken Bon Jovi way beyond the boundaries of American culture. Their influence is global and has been since their first tour in the '80s. They have been smart enough to understand that a band cannot be universally popular all the time. There is some give and take, "and the truth is, this is our first tour of South America in fifteen years, and we didn't come for fifteen years because the records didn't do as well here as they did in America. It's not that we have this planetary appeal, that when every record comes out, you are that big, everywhere. Europe turns its back on you for certain records and then embraces others, as does America."[11]

The continuous touring to every corner of the globe has endeared the band to fans all over the world. In the documentary *When We Were Beautiful*, the band is in Abu Dhabi, London, Dublin, Munich, and New York while touring the *Lost Highway* album (at the time, the band had yet to visit Israel or Greece). Audiences that see the band perform live in their own countries have a direct connection to Bon Jovi. The band becomes relevant to their lives. Fans are not just hearing songs on the radio; they are seeing the band live, and looking forward to seeing them again in the future. Of course, this is why Bon Jovi revisits locations. A satisfied fan is a paying fan.

International touring is not as simple as making hotel reservations. For an outfit like Bon Jovi it involves all kinds of permits, arrangements, travel documents, timetables, and massive coordination. They dealt with political and social roadblocks early in their touring career. They were one of the first rock bands to perform in St. Petersburg, Russia, in the '80s, and in 2009 they performed "We Weren't Born to Follow" at an event commemorating the twentieth anniversary of the fall of the Berlin Wall.

When considering the many trips the band has made over the years to certain countries, it is possible that they have visited some places more times than heads of state. When visiting some countries, Bon Jovi may be the best representative America has. It is in this capacity that Bon Jovi, and many other rock bands, serve as kind of unofficial ambassadors of America to the world at large. Rock bands of the 20th and 21st centuries may turn out to be America's saving grace when it comes to our reputation around the world. They certainly have done more to engage foreign countries' goodwill than any politicians of late history. If people on other continents have good feelings about America, they may well be due to ambassadors of rock. As one Australian attempts to describe Bon Jovi's popularity, it is possible to imagine the people of any continent saying the same things: "People love Bon Jovi . . . we're talking crazy, devoted, favourite-band-ever kind of love."[12]

TOURING AS BRAND PROMOTION

Whether it was the *modus operandi* of their early manager, Doc McGhee, the requirement of the record label, or Jon Bon Jovi's foresight as to what it takes to make a thirty-year career, Bon Jovi toured relentlessly through their first four albums. They have since toured more than most bands and with deliberate marketing strategies in mind. In various interviews, members of the band have discussed how physically and emotionally draining the early tours were. They often would go months without a real break. As a group, Bon Jovi agrees that the band almost broke up for good after a particularly rough long-term tour in the early '90s. Richie Sambora has an opinion about why the band's album *Slippery When Wet* was successful and the part touring played: "We toured them so diligently, it was old time hockey. I think we shoved them down everybody's throat."[13] It may have been "old time hockey," but it worked. The very act of touring makes a band culturally relevant. Live performance is a completely different experience than listening to a band's music on the radio or an album. The act of a band coming to where the fans are and performing live makes the band real and relevant.

When Bon Jovi hits the road, it is with a huge staff of hundreds of individuals and massive equipment of all kinds. Everyone has to work together and be coordinated to run a professional organization that puts on great concerts. Jon Bon Jovi relies heavily on his trusted inner circle of staff, like Paul Korzilius and others at AEG and Creative Artists Agency (CAA). A huge part of the success of an international tour is choosing the best places to go, and that requires business savvy. The tour management team carefully selects the routes and cities of the tour. No one knows how important this process is more than Jon Bon Jovi. It is a fine balance of meeting fan demands and knowing when to go where. He knows the market can be fickle: "We're aware that you have to keep a presence in places or you'll lose that following."[14]

In addition to the planning of routes, the marketing is specified for each location. The press, retail goods, radio, Internet, and what happens before and after a concert are planned and carried out according to the specific market. For all these reasons, Bon Jovi has never had to "rely on one marketplace to distribute" their records.[15]

The band's most recent tour, Because We Can, started in February of 2013 and will span the globe with performance dates. Bon Jovi is bringing new technology to their tour, with a specially designed app that highlights interactive art from the album to reveal tour-themed music and videos to the user. In addition, the band is making a concerted effort to make concerts accessible by offering seven levels of pricing to the public, including a $19.50 price point. Considering that the average ticket price for the Slippery When Wet Tour in 1986 was $16.50, it's a bargain.

THE DOCUMENTARY FILM AS SELF-PROMOTION

There is a scene filmed in black and white in the 2009 Bon Jovi documentary *When We Were Beautiful* in which a pensive and serious Jon Bon Jovi is sitting alone in a beach-toned hotel room. He is on the phone, speaking with a mysterious mover and shaker about possible ownership of an NFL team. In shorts and no shoes, he is poised in front of a white Apple computer, looking at a packed schedule as he tries to find a time to meet with the person on the phone. He sums up his pitch with: "I'm the CEO of a major corporation who has been running a brand for twenty-five years."[16]

The Phil Griffin–directed documentary debuted at the Tribeca Film Festival in April of 2009 and was available on Showtime for a limited time. The title of the film is the name of a track off *The Circle*. Until the documentary was released, many people may have not been aware of how the business of Bon Jovi is conducted. The documentary is a telling peek inside the empire of Bon Jovi, Inc. Most insiders who know the man and the band seem to agree that Jon Bon Jovi's business acumen is formidable. The fact that Jon Bon Jovi views the band that bears his name as a brand speaks to how he views his enterprise. The documentary reveals a group of men who do not resemble their younger selves. The wide-eyed, enthusiastic New Jersey dreamers we had a glimpse of in the videos of the late '80s are gone. In their place are four men who have been through a lot of life's experiences and bear the war wounds. One band member who was with them through the early successful years, Alec John Such, is not included in the documentary at all.

There is no question that Jon Bon Jovi is the master of the sound bite. He does not miss an opportunity to build up his brand in public. Whether he is speaking with a member of the media or a high-profile interviewer on national television, he usually comes off as decent and highly professional. He regularly interjects facts about the band's record sales and history into whatever questions he is being asked. It isn't enough for him to be interviewed; he wants to remind the public why the band is as successful as is it. The documentary is no exception. In a media meet and greet immediately prior to the Concert in Central Park in 2008, Jon casually mentioned the biggest names in music that have performed there and shares that "somehow they let a rock band in here."[17] He pulls it off as a humble comment, but he has clearly given a great deal of thought to what he was going to say. It couldn't have been scripted better.

The documentary offers a few reveals. David Bryan shares that all is not perfect in Joviland, but it is "not bad enough to walk away." He also mentions that Jon is on Prozac ("or whatever he's on"). Tico Torres is remarkably introspective and is open about the fact that his alcoholism was made worse by a bad relationship with his father. Jon reveals that Tico used to be a "mean, mean man" when he drank. Richie Sambora is quite open about "being broken" and his personal problems, but manages to come across as a decent and humble kind of person.[18] The audience finds out that Tico and Richie knew a lot of the same women in the old days and that Jon's hair is going gray. We get a peek into the VIP treatment that Jon receives on the road (a private chiropractor/ massage therapist before a show, a car and driver immediately back-stage after a stadium show to whisk him away to the hotel, the backstage staff waiting with bated breath for his decision about the night's set list and then running it to the rest of the crew before the show—and there is much more). Jon Bon Jovi himself admitted that he wanted to keep control over what was released in the film: "We wanted to document what this is all about and keep creative control."[19] The extent of this control is that there is very little commentary from anyone not in the band. Kid Rock provides some hero worship, but that is about it.

What the documentary shows us is that Bon Jovi is still relevant to the music industry and audiences. On the Lost Highway Tour (and any other), the band employs hundreds of music industry workers to make the tour happen in an age when it is hard to find work of any kind. Watching the band perform at Madison Square Garden in the film, it is impossible to ignore the fact that they are still very popular; there are just so many people in attendance. This band still draws huge audi-ences. In New York City, Jon Bon Jovi gives a press conference with Mayor Michael Bloomberg to promote the Concert in Central Park. The project brought the two men together out of necessity, but it is significant to note that Bon Jovi has access to an extremely influential top politician in one of the most important cities in the world.

Bon Jovi enjoyed a sort of media blitz in 2010, following the 2009 debut of the *When We Were Beautiful* documentary on Showtime. The coffee table book of the same name was published, The Circle Tour was in full force, and a *Greatest Hits* album was released during the tour. The band was first to perform from the roof of the O2 arena in London and performed at the Grammys. The documentary and frenetic activity of 2010 resulted in Bon Jovi making up a large part of the discussion in the music industry that year. Their presence permeated several aspects of culture; in fact, most Americans probably saw their image or heard their music in 2010. The tour grossed $201.1 million, making it the top music tour of the year.

Rob Light of the CAA talent agency describes the relevancy of mar-keting: "Marketing starts with the artists themselves, and Jon is probably one of the smartest, most savvy artists in the world in terms of working it."[20] Jon Bon Jovi has crafted a solid brand over a thirty-year career by using his instincts, talent, and business acumen. He has achieved the gold standard that is brand recognition.

8

PHILANTHROPY—BON JOVI'S OTHER LEGACY

Philanthropic work is not usually expected of a rock band. Perhaps this is why there is more attention paid to a celebrity's charity. Our society seems to pay more attention to causes that are endorsed by someone famous. It may be an obsession with celebrity or just a response to someone pointing toward a worthy cause. One example of a rock band taking philanthropy to a heightened level is U2. Increasingly in the past two decades, lead singer Bono has incorporated politically motivated speeches and images into the band's concert format; he has also started the charity organization known as the ONE foundation, whose mission includes anti-poverty and anti-disease initiatives. Similarly, Bon Jovi seems to have done more than their share of charitable outreach and professional philanthropy, both collectively and as individuals. In comparing the two bands, there is a disparity between how they are respected for their philanthropic work and their music. U2 has always done very well with music critics, and has received a huge amount of publicity for their charity work (mostly Bono). Bono is often photographed with political and social leaders all over the globe as a serious player on the philanthropic stage. In contrast, Bon Jovi has historically not done well with music critics and has not received the same level of attention as Bono when it comes to charitable outreach. For example, Bono has been nominated for a Nobel Peace Prize and been made an honorary knight of the British Empire. One possible reason for this is that Bon Jovi is focused on improving mostly domestic social issues, while U2 focuses on international issues. Another reason may be that Bon Jovi's music is considered less serious than U2's music, and therefore Jon Bon Jovi's charitable pursuits are not as worthy of attention as Bono's. Another possibility is that U2 is an international, European band, and throughout the world this gives them a certain validation and credibility that an American band does not have.

Bon Jovi's charity outreach most likely began, and has continued, in their home state of New Jersey. Whether through an event held to help the families of fallen police and fire heroes, to benefit sick children, or to save a historic performance venue, Bon Jovi has stepped up, along with others, and given their time for the greater good. In more recent years, the band has worked collectively on various philanthropic projects (9/11 aftermath, Superstorm Sandy), and they have also pursued their interests as individuals in giving back to their communities and the world at large. Their New Jersey work ethic and big hearts have endeared the band to those who may not have been music fans and have also enabled Jon, Richie, David, and Tico to help people on a larger scale than they most likely ever imagined.

SEPTEMBER 11, 2001

The most devastating terrorist attacks ever to take place on American soil happened on September 11, 2001, in New York City, Washington, D.C., and Shanksville, Pennsylvania. Jon Bon Jovi and Richie Sambora experienced these events and emotions along with the rest of the greater New York area. The pair was working on an album at Bon Jovi's home at the time of the attacks. His county in New Jersey was one of the hardest hit in the state in terms of human loss. Jon Bon Jovi's home on the Navesink River had direct views of smoke wafting from New York City.

Bon Jovi's studio album *Bounce* was shaped by the events of September 11. The lyrics were a direct reflection of what people were feeling and thinking in the months following the attacks. Jon Bon Jovi explains: "This is not a 9/11 record, but had I not made any reference to what happened on that day I would have been remiss . . . I live in New Jersey. The smoke was wafting over my house, the towers were burning in front of me and my community was affected."[1] The song "Undivided" mentions how Jon "found courage in the smoke and dust." Bon Jovi are not the only musicians artistically influenced by the events of 9/11: others include Tori Amos, Toby Keith, Will Smith, Mary J. Blige, Bruce Springsteen, Slayer, Rush, and Fleetwood Mac, to name just a few.

As a band and residents of New Jersey and New York, Bon Jovi participated in many charity events in remembrance of fallen police officers, firemen, and emergency workers of 9/11. By all accounts, like many other celebrities, they wanted to support and highlight the work of blue-collar emergency workers who made a difference that horrible day. Events included America: A Tribute to Heroes; the Twin Towers Relief Benefit; the 9/11 Relief Alliance of Neighbors; and, most famously, the Concert for New York City, held at Madison Square Garden in October of 2001. Some of the biggest names in music performed at the event, including Paul McCartney, Keith Richards, Mick Jagger, Pete Townshend, Billy Joel, Eric Clapton, Elton John, David Bowie, James Taylor, Bon Jovi, and many others. The concert raised $14 million in ticket sales, and many other millions in donations, CD sales, and corporate support. Later in 2001, another concert took place to benefit the Alliance of Neighbors of Monmouth County. The alliance's main purpose was to financially assist victims of the 9/11 attacks. Many of the same bands mentioned above participated, and almost half a million dollars was raised. Jon Bon Jovi followed up on his promise not to forget 9/11 when he performed in a show in honor of emergency workers who put their lives at risk to save others. The show, broadcast in 2011, marked the ten-year anniversary of 9/11. All of these events financially benefitted survivors and families of the attacks, but they also served as a positive and essential experience of community for the general public trying to cope.

BON JOVI'S OUTREACH

It is interesting to consider what the impetus is that motivates a person to give back to his community by performing charitable works. It may be a relationship with someone who inspires or influences an individual. In the case of someone as privileged as Jon Bon Jovi and the rest of his band, it may be the feeling of responsibility that can come with having so much. The band was unexpectedly indoctrinated into outreach early in their career. It was enforced outreach in the form of anti-drug rallies and performances, as part of a court-mandated punishment for the drug smuggling activities of their manager, Doc McGhee. In the end, it was most likely a mixed blessing, in the sense that the anti-drug outreach forced them to confront philanthropy as an important part of being famous much earlier in their career then they otherwise would have. There is no doubt that, over the years, the band has been approached many, many times to be a part of all kinds of charitable events and initiatives.

As an organization, Bon Jovi has always done their part in helping others. They are one of the only bands to run a charitable promotion tied in with ticket sales. As part of The Circle Tour in 2010, front row seats were sold at a greatly reduced price to members of the Backstage with Bon Jovi fan club, and a large portion of that ticket revenue went to Jon's Soul Foundation. In the grand American tradition of getting something for a charitable donation, individuals could feel good about purchasing these tickets. The result was that each concert directly benefitted people in need. Jon Bon Jovi usually makes sure that the Soul Foundation has some kind of a presence at concerts, and it is not unusual to see a Soul Foundation banner or materials.

As a band, they have performed at many charitable events, including events to benefit the Greater Boston Food Bank, the Elton John AIDS Foundation, and AIDS Project Los Angeles; the Rainforest Foundation Benefit Concert; A Very Special Christmas from Washington, D.C.; A Celebration of Special Olympics; Live Earth; and Apollo Theater Fundraiser.

Bon Jovi has also reached out to friends in need. One example is when longtime manager Paul Korzilius's daughter was murdered. Nancy and Paul Korzilius's six-year-old daughter, Katherine Korzilius, was found dead on a public street on August 7, 1996, minutes after her mother had dropped her off at the mailbox, trusting her to walk the quarter-mile home in safety. She never made it. Her death remains unexplained, and while hit-and-run seems a common theory, the physical evidence does not support this idea. Her mother has said she believes that someone laid her daughter out on the street, arranged her so she looked at peace, and for this reason fully believes the girl suffered a wrongful death.[2] Jon Bon Jovi responded to the horrific event by trying to express his emotion in a song titled "August 7th 4:15," the time of Katherine's death.

In 2005, the band appeared on *The Oprah Winfrey Show* to promote their new album, *Have a Nice Day*. The appearance included an in-depth interview with Jon Bon Jovi about his personal life and philanthropic work. It also included a surprise $1 million donation to Oprah's Angel Network (her largest donation to date). The donation was equally made by Jon Bon Jovi, Richie Sambora, David Bryan, and Tico Torres and was intended to help efforts in the Hurricane Katrina cleanup.

GIVING BACK TO JERSEY

Bon Jovi owes much of their success to New Jersey. Not only because their home state has always been incredibly supportive of them, but also because the area and people of Asbury Park provided a community and multiple venues for them to learn their craft. Because of that, the band has always been more than willing to step in when needed. They still have relationships with musicians they knew from the Jersey Shore, and personal relationships have inspired the band to reach out to help when called upon. One such calling was the Come Together concert that took place in 1998 for the purpose of raising funds for the Sgt. Patrick King Memorial Fund. Sgt. King was killed in the line of duty and left behind a family that needed financial support. Jon Bon Jovi organized the event. Performing musicians included all of Bon Jovi (with Hugh McDonald), Southside Johnny and some of the Asbury Jukes, Bobby Bandiera, Little Steven (van Zandt), Bruce Springsteen, Patti Scialfa, Max Weinberg, Clarence Clemons, and many others. Asbury Park native Danny DeVito served as the master of ceremonies.

In 2003, the Hope Concert benefit took place for the purpose of raising money for Bobby Bandiera's family, specifically for Bob Bandiera Jr., who was in need of financial assistance. This event later became known as the Bobby Bandiera All-Star Holiday Concert. Subsequent Hope concerts benefitted the Valerie Fund Children's Center at the Children's Hospital at Monmouth Medical Center and the Parker Family Health Center in Red Bank, New Jersey.

The generosity of the musicians and people who attended the concerts had a direct positive effect on both those in need and all the people of the concentrated geographic area of eastern New Jersey. The band not only has a deeply ingrained work ethic from their New Jersey roots, but also a strong sense of taking care of their own. The fact that the Hope series of concerts directly helped New Jersey citizens was the impetus for band participation.

Hurricane Sandy, the massive storm that hit the East Coast in 2012, caused billions of dollars in damage and much destruction to parts of New York and New Jersey. Similar to the rush of charitable activity that occurred after 9/11, the music industry came together to raise money to repair the damage. The concert was titled 12-12-12 and took place at Madison Square Garden. The performing lineup included rock royalty such as the Rolling Stones, Billy Joel, Paul McCartney, Eddie Vedder, Alicia Keys, Bruce Springsteen, and, of course, Bon Jovi. Several members of the band were personally affected by the storm. David Bryan lost a house, Jon Bon Jovi's family was stranded in New York City without heat or power, and Richie Sambora's mother had serious flooding in her Point Pleasant home and had to move in with her son. Jon Bon Jovi continued to support the cause by serving on the Hurricane Sandy New Jersey Relief Fund.

JON BON JOVI

As a philanthropist Jon Bon Jovi has an impeccable record and a reputation that is more solid and respectable than most politicians. He possesses enough self-awareness to realize that his presence at an event can draw much-needed attention to a cause. He is willing to be self-exploitive to add something of value to a charitable effort. For example, at Bon Jovi's 2005 appearance on *The Oprah Winfrey Show*, his reason for being there was to promote his new album, but he also made a surprise visit to a fan at her home bearing pink roses; donated money to the Angel Network; and showed a video of his visit to Philadelphia's Northern Home for Children. The exposure of the orphanage's struggles and efforts alerted the public to the serious social issue of unwanted and disadvantaged children. He managed to cover business, philanthropy, and fun in one commercial-interrupted hour.

His work with organizations like Special Olympics, the American Red Cross, City of Hope, the Elizabeth Glaser Pediatric AIDS Foundation, and Habitat for Humanity (named first-ever ambassador for the organization) was instrumental in the ultimate development of his own organization. His commitment to philanthropy is so impressive that it was formally recognized by President Barack Obama, who hand-selected Jon to serve on the Committee for Community Solutions in 2012. He was formally recognized with the Humanitarian Award at the 2008 Billboard Touring Awards.

Jon has discussed how his idea to reach out to the homeless came from an experience he had one winter night in the city of Philadelphia, looking out his hotel room window. He recalls: "I saw a homeless man sleeping on the steps of city hall . . . and I thought, 'this isn't what our forefathers were thinking when they drafted the constitution.' This is not the way it was supposed to be in Philadelphia."[3] For Jon, this defining moment spurred him on to the next phase of his professional and personal life.

Jon Bon Jovi Soul Foundation

When Sister Mary Scullion was asked whether or not Jon Bon Jovi was a "good" Catholic boy, she replied, "He is the *best* Catholic boy."[4] These are strong words coming from a nun. Sister Mary would know more than most from her service on the Jon Bon Jovi Soul Foundation Board of Directors. As one of the founders, in 1989, of Philadelphia's Project HOME, she taught Jon much about how to work with others and how to address the needs of a community. Jon's nonprofit organization was founded in 2006 and was formerly named the Philadelphia Soul Charitable Foundation when it was a supporting organization of the Philadelphia Soul football team owned by Bon Jovi and Craig Spencer. The Soul football team was not any ordinary sports organization. From the start, the intention of the owners was that everyone involved in the organization, from the players to the staff, would contribute to the greater good of the Philadelphia community, where they were based. If a team member was not contributing positively, he was no longer part of the Soul. Jon and the Soul coach, Mike Trigg, employed a "no thug" rule in hiring players. Jon describes how the organization found out a player was selling his team T-shirt on eBay. When he complained about the living quarters ("I don't room with nobody"), the organization replied, "You're right, you're not rooming with anybody. Get out."[5]

The Soul's community relations mission statement is singular. There has certainly never been anything like it in professional sports. It reads in part: "The Philadelphia Soul organization is dedicated to enriching the lives of underprivileged children, teens, and adults in the city of Philadelphia."[6] Among the projects the Soul accomplished are the following: provided beds to Covenant House in Philadelphia, built a playground for the Northern Home for Children orphanage, and made significant financial donations to local Philadelphia charities including the Corporate Alliance for Drug Education (CADE), Philadelphia Children's Alliance, Philabundance, Inn Dwelling, Project HOME, Second Floor Youth Helpline, and the Delaware Valley Adoption Center. They provided free tickets so children could attend a Soul game and coordinated and followed through many charity drives, including teddy bears for abused children (Philadelphia Children's Alliance), new and used books for Philadelphia Reads, and school supplies for Northern Home for Children.

A more recent example of the type of project the JBJ Soul Foundation is undertaking is a collaboration with Philadelphia's Northern Children's Services. The purpose of the project is to expand their housing facilities to include permanent housing for homeless teenage mothers and children. Besides the JBJ Soul Foundation, Wawa, Inc., is also a supporter of the project. The Soul Foundation made a $100,000 commitment to support the initiative. This is only one example of the hundreds of units of affordable housing the Foundation has made possible.

The devastation of Hurricane Katrina brought out the worst in many Americans, including then First Lady Barbara Bush. Her abhorrent comment on the state of the evacuees in the Houston Astrodome was widely publicized because of its inflammatory nature. She stated that many of the evacuees she had seen were better off than they had been prior to the storm. She went on to say that "they all want to stay in Texas" and that the evacuees were "underprivileged anyway, so this is working very well for them."[7] Unlike Mrs. Bush, the Soul Foundation chose to focus on immediate needs rather than socioeconomic and racial issues, and concentrated on getting people in homes as soon as possible. Within one year, "Bon Jovi Boulevard" existed in Houma, Louisiana. Bon Jovi has said: "The thing I'm proudest of, the one-year anniversary, those twenty-eight people were in their homes. By cracking the whip, yelling, finger-pointing—we got it done."[8] The band, working with Oprah's Angel Network and the Bayou Area Habitat for Humanity, sponsored twenty-eight homes in the Bayou Blue Community. All the homes went to victims of the hurricane.

One indication of how Jon Bon Jovi's concept of his own legacy has changed was evident on his 2010 world tour. The tour included visits by Jon Bon Jovi to local homeless organizations to gather ideas for how to improve his own organization, the Jon Bon Jovi Soul Foundation. When asked why he was focusing on the issue of homelessness, Jon responded: "There's just more to be said and done, and the difference that can be felt on the trail that you've made."[9]

The Soul Kitchen

The Soul Kitchen is an offshoot of the JBJ Soul Foundation, and it is a personal project for Jon Bon Jovi. His wife, Dorothea, has taken an active role in the creation and operation of the restaurant, and they both regularly volunteer their time when possible. All proceeds from the restaurant go to charities related to the Soul Foundation or wherever they are most needed. The restaurant's location in Red Bank, New Jersey, is close to the Bon Jovis' home and near the Count Basie Theatre, where Jon has performed many times over the years. The area is very close to Asbury Park, a place where Jon Bon Jovi virtually grew up as a musician and performer.

The idea was to create a place where anyone can eat delicious food and where people having a challenging financial time can get a good meal in exchange for their service (not their money). This arrangement avoids the stigma of a food or soup kitchen, and empowers people who need help. Jon Bon Jovi elaborates on the concept of helping yourself: "This is not an entitlement thing. This is about empowering people because you have to earn that certificate."[10] Those customers who are able to pay leave whatever amount they feel is appropriate in an envelope on the table, and there are no food prices listed on the menu. It is also possible for individuals to volunteer at another local outreach facility, like the local food bank, and receive a certificate for a meal at the Soul Kitchen.

Jon and Dorothea's initiative and willingness to start the restaurant brings a depth of validity to Bon Jovi at large. It would be so much easier to write a check and let someone else create it, but they did the work, found the right project and location, and made it happen. The direct result of their work is a repurposed building that has been completely renovated to meld with the surrounding area; a thriving, self-sustaining vegetable garden for chefs to use at the restaurant; and an attractive place where hungry people can get food. Red Bank is off the beaten path, but will find more people coming to the town to support the Kitchen. When asked about the benefits of people paying for food, volunteer Justin said: "I think it makes people feel better about themselves."[11]

Charitable Enterprise

Jon Bon Jovi has managed to find a way to combine charity, fashion, and couture fragrance. Bon Jovi and fashion designer Kenneth Cole created a very special advertising campaign centered around a charitable cause. In early 2007, the two men launched the Kenneth Cole fragrance RSVP in conjunction with Coty, Inc., in an effort to benefit several organizations committed to helping homeless people, specifically Habitat for Humanity, HELP USA, and the Philadelphia Soul Charitable Foundation. The kickoff included a red carpet event in Tribeca, New York City, and a silent and live auction to raise money for the organizations. Items up for auction included a private golf lesson with Tiger Woods, vacations to the Caribbean, and a custom 2007 Saturn vehicle. Coty, Inc., pledged $1 million toward the cause. Jon Bon Jovi performed an acoustic set that featured the song "Who Says You Can't Go Home" (which was also featured in the commercial for the RSVP fragrance).

The RSVP project was not Cole and Bon Jovi's first collaboration. They produced a limited-edition outerwear collection in October of 2006 that was available at Kenneth Cole stores and Saks Fifth Avenue. Both the RSVP to Help project and Coty fragrance (under the auspices of Lancaster Group US LLC) are "Build Partners" of Jon Bon Jovi's Soul Foundation. Donations at this level are set at the amount of $100,000 or more.

RICHIE SAMBORA

Richie Sambora has served as a fund-raiser for various charities, which include the Steve Young Forever Young Foundation and Stand Up for a Cure. He has also been a big supporter of the Michael J. Fox Foundation, which has raised an amazing $300 million toward a cure for Parkinson's disease. He has made donations to hospitals where his late father received cancer treatment, Memorial Sloan-Kettering and MD Anderson hospitals.

Richie Sambora started the You Can Go Home program in his hometown of Woodbridge, New Jersey, and donated funds to his alma mater, Woodbridge High School. The school created a new weight room named the Adam Sambora Fitness Center in honor of Richie's father. Sambora was recognized with the Golden Heart Award for his work with the Midnight Mission charity in 2012.

TICO TORRES

Tico Torres has created the Tico Torres Children Foundation for the purpose of assisting children in need. The Foundation is committed to putting at least eighty percent of their donations directly toward children's needs. In early 2010, the Foundation organized an effort to aid children in Haiti in need of health care by working with HOMS hospitals (Dominican Republic), Global Care Delivery, Inc., and a large network of international doctors. Torres has continued his commitment to helping children in need by participating in Celebrities Fore Kids with Jack Nicklaus in November of 2012. The golf charity event raised money for children in need of cancer treatment.

DAVID BRYAN

David Rashbaum Bryan is committed to helping children by serving as an honorary board member of the Only Make Believe organization. Similarly, he serves as a national representative of VH1's Save the Music Foundation. This well-established foundation's purpose is to improve the quality of music education in America. Bryan recently donated a Steinway concert grand piano to the U.S. Department of State in Washington, D.C.

A lifetime of touring the globe and observing the suffering of different types of people has given Bon Jovi a truly unique perspective on philanthropy. As they have aged and refocused their priorities, the band members have carefully selected which charitable causes they want to put their efforts toward. By using their celebrity status to draw attention where help is required, the band has improved individuals' lives and communities in the United States and beyond.

Bon Jovi's best legacy may be their philanthropic work. By sharing their wealth with those less fortunate, giving their time to set an example, and instigating change where they see a need, they have created a model of excellence for other American bands to follow.

JON BON JOVI AS POLITICAL ACTIVIST

Jon Bon Jovi's astute business sense, humble blue-collar beginning, and access to some of the world's most wealthy individuals have made him into a person who understands the connection between politics and philanthropy. His skills and attributes also put him in the unique position of having an influence on American politics. His political activism has come to life through his support of several Democratic political candidates, his appointment to a White House community solutions think tank, and his passionate work to eliminate homelessness.

In the political arena, he has publicly supported John Kerry in his bid for the presidency, Al Gore's candidacy and his work for environmental causes, Hillary Clinton in her efforts to eliminate her campaign debt as a senator, and presidential candidate Barack Obama during both elections.

During John Kerry's 2004 presidential campaign, Jon Bon Jovi toured with and performed on behalf of the John Kerry and John Edwards ticket by serenading students on college campuses and speaking to them about the importance of casting their votes. Earlier in the decade (2000) he went on the road to support Al Gore. He performed at a party at the vice president's (Al Gore) home the night he made his concession speech to George Bush. Bon Jovi has served as something of a de facto music star or "troubadour" of the Democratic party for the last several years, coming to Washington, D.C., to perform and schmooze at various fund-raisers, parties, and gatherings. His presence and publicity in publications such as the *Washington Post* tie him to many politicians, lawmakers, and policy wonks. They are drawn to his guitar and rock star persona like moths to the flame. There is no denying that he has the ear of important D.C. insiders; Jon Bon Jovi is in a position to influence public policy.

In January of 2009, Jon Bon Jovi headlined a concert at Town Hall in Manhattan to raise money to erase Hillary Clinton's presidential campaign debt. The event was called "Thank You, Hillary: A Salute to Hillary Clinton," and ticket prices ranged from $75 to $1,000.

He was a strong supporter of Barack Obama's first presidential campaign, in 2008, performing live at the We Are One inaugural concert on the steps of the Lincoln Memorial, and he championed for him again during the second Obama campaign, in 2012. Bon Jovi generated much press when the president gave him a ride from Washington, D.C., to New York City in June of 2012 on Air Force One. He was on his way to perform at a fund-raising party for the president at the Waldorf Astoria hotel.

During Obama's first campaign (2008), the Bon Jovi family hosted a private dinner at their home in New Jersey to raise money for his election ($30,800 per person for dinner). The money raised supported the Obama Victory Fund in conjunction with the Democratic National Committee. Governor Jon Corzine served as co-host. Bon Jovi's personal touch of opening his home for the benefit of Obama certainly endeared Jon to the First Family. It is a relationship that has been maintained through the years.

Jon Bon Jovi has said, "I don't know that I would have had the same entrée to Presidential politics had I not been as successful in my day job."[12] There is most certainly no doubt that this is a true statement. As in the way of Frank Sinatra, Elvis Presley, Marilyn Monroe, or any other celebrity who has access to the Office of the President, Jon is in a position to start a conversation solely because of his celebrity status. Even his money and vision as a philanthropist are secondary to the fact that he is extremely famous. As is typical in American culture, the fact that he is famous is exponentially more important than the reason he is famous.

Bon Jovi's efforts were rewarded (or punished, depending on your view) with a 2012 presidential appointment under the honorary chairmanship of First Lady Michelle Obama.

Bon Jovi's appointment is not a vanity post, nor a thank you for personal campaign donations, as he is uniquely qualified to participate on a council whose main purpose is to "identify resources to help our nation's young people succeed."[13] His prolific outreach work with homeless youth and his own four children qualify him to serve. What is most intriguing about the Council is not Bon Jovi's participation on it, but the fact that he claims to have come up with the idea himself: "In 2008, like so many others I was inspired by Obama . . . I wrote to the White House shortly after the election to suggest a council on volunteerism. After some thought they suggested the White House Council for Community Solutions and offered me a seat."[14] Since he joined the Council, Jon Bon Jovi has been one of the most visible members to the public. One of the outreach goals of the Council is "listening efforts" to better understand challenged youth and community collaborations. One such listening tour took place in New Orleans in 2011. Café Reconcile is a restaurant in New Orleans that teaches youth marketable skills for future employment and opportunity. In a video of the event, Jon Bon Jovi is seen standing in the shadows, intently listening to a teenager. He says, "The kids here want to be heard," and the young people are nodding their heads. There seems to be a genuine connection between Bon Jovi and the youth. Another stop on the tour in June of 2011 was in Newark, New Jersey, at the Rutgers Youth Education and Employment Success Center. Jon made an impression on the young people there: "He seemed like he really wanted to help us resolve the issues. And that's what made it really good."[15]

The response that Jon receives from people he meets on outreach missions appears to be truly positive. The youth, for example, felt a truthfulness in his intentions that cannot be denied. It takes a special person to cross socioeconomic and racial boundaries to communicate honestly and freely with different people. While Jon has begun well, it remains to be seen whether he has the ability to make real change happen for the Council's programs. Jon and the other Council members who attended these events will present their findings to the president's administration.

Bon Jovi seems to be getting much out of his experiences with the Council. Even though his presidential appointment is a direct result of his involvement in Obama's campaign, he insists that the assignment is not political. "I get great pleasure, pride, and joy in giving back. I'm very proud to be part of this President's council, and just to underscore, it's not political, but I really feel at fifty years old, I should do other things than sing in a rock and roll band." [16]

Jon's most important political work may be his fight to eliminate homelessness. In his typical blue-chip style, he went out and found the absolute best mentor possible to help him establish skills and credibility in this arena: Sister Mary Scullion. At the helm of Philadelphia's Project HOME she created a national model of how to eliminate homelessness, and she helped shape what the Soul Foundation is today. Their relationship is one of mutual admiration. It has been said that Bon Jovi's anthem to the underdog, "We Weren't Born to Follow," has a tribute line to Sister Mary. The lyrics "this one goes out to the one who does it differently, this one is for the one who curses and spits" supposedly describe the unconventional nun. About Sister Mary, Jon has said, "It was Sister Mary who taught me the importance of job training and service providing. These elements were going to be key to the success in and around each of our builds." [17]

The Jon Bon Jovi Soul Foundation and Soul Kitchen are two organizations clearly established with the intention of philanthropic outreach, but they are also political stages on which Bon Jovi can stand. His commitment to helping others, and his substantial financial contributions, give him a certain authenticity in starting a conversation about social change with just about anyone. With the high profile of the Foundation (enforced by the Bon Jovi fan base and a successful record), Jon Bon Jovi is in a position to use the Foundation to question a presidential candidate about social change, ask a sitting president what Washington, D.C., is doing about homelessness, or suggest that other wealthy individuals start their own Soul Kitchen. Basically, he can shake things up quite a bit. In this age of digital connections and social media, he is poised to make some kind of impression on the general public. For example, former President Bill Clinton has already visited the Soul Kitchen in Red Bank, New Jersey, as an unofficial endorsement of Jon's good works. The official purpose of the visit was to fulfill an auction win for the 100 Women in Hedge Funds Gala.

As a presidential appointee to the White House Council for Community Solutions as well as the chairman of the Soul Foundation, Jon Bon Jovi was invited to participate in the 2012 Health Datapalooza, sponsored by the Institute of Medicine of the National Academies and the U.S. Department of Health and Human Services. Bon Jovi told the story of a man who worked at the Soul Kitchen very late because he had nowhere to go. Because of a lack of personal resources he could not find a place to stay. It was this story and many others just like it that led to the development of apps that assist the homeless. Jon sought to find "a technology solution for community care-givers and others to find shelters that have open spaces on a real-time basis." Two new apps that the Soul Foundation are piloting are "Homeless Helper" and "Help Beacon." An individual or care-giver looking for a place for a homeless person to sleep can find an available bed in real time by using the apps.

Jon Bon Jovi's appealing persona, popularity, wealth, connections, drive, and political views beg the question of whether he is fit to run for public office. He is certainly more genuine and committed to helping others than many politicians today (has any member of Congress started a free restaurant?). Bon Jovi is posed this question in most interviews about his political activism, and in responding he looks flattered and says he is not interested in such a pursuit. Why would he be? Right now, he can do anything he wants without the annoyance of satisfying constituents, and make a significant difference in people's lives, on his own terms. He speaks of his organization as "we": "we can do more philanthropically than being elected to office."[18] Most would agree that this is certainly true. The most noble aspect of being in political office is helping people in need, and Bon Jovi can do this now without pause. Another reason he will not run for office may also have to do with living the "rock star lifestyle" for a few years in the mid-1980s. When asked if he had any skeletons in his closet, he replied, "I couldn't run for political office, let's put it that way."[19]

EPILOGUE

Bon Jovi Forever

David Bryan has said about Bon Jovi, "It's a relationship closer than marriage. You know, we can't divorce each other . . . the only way out of this band, I think, is death."[1] Of course, they could divorce each other if they really wanted to, but it would mean a premature end to what is lining up to be a Rolling Stones type of career. The band has survived a decades-long career in a music industry that has evolved through unprecedented change. For example, when Bon Jovi started in 1983, records were still vinyl and there was no Internet. Digital music did not exist and you could see a rock concert for under fifty dollars. No one had heard of rap, hip-hop, or grunge musical styles. Today, digital downloads are the way most people purchase music, radio airplay is so heavily programmed that a breakout record is impossible, and many will pay well over $1,000 for a concert ticket.

Their stadium rock and universal lyrics have sustained them through every music trend of the past thirty years. They delved into a country-influenced record that many people thought was the end of the band, and later came back even stronger with a return to stadium rock on *The Circle* and *What About Now?* albums.

The band survived the loss of their founding bass player, Alec John Such, and moved on very well with *Keep the Faith* in 1992. There has never been a clear explanation of how Such's departure came about, but in a *RAW* interview in 1994, Such said, "I decided not to be on the record—and it was my decision."² In the same interview, Such claims that he was not allowed to speak to the press during previous world tours, and he was banned from doing so by Jon Bon Jovi. No solid information has been made public as to whether Such was fired or left the band voluntarily, and even on Oprah's *Master Class* series Jon did not reveal anything of substance about the matter.

The band shows no signs of slowing down. Their 2013 activities include the Because We Can tour and the release of the *What About Now?* album. Richie Sambora released his third solo album, titled *Aftermath of the Lowdown*, in 2012; David Bryan is working on a new musical, which will be in workshop at La Jolla Playhouse in 2013; Tico Torres is active as owner of the children's clothing and accessories line Rock Star Baby; and Jon Bon Jovi is serving on President Obama's White House Council for Community Solutions and continuing to write songs for films.

Bon Jovi has become a part of American culture because of their popular success and longevity, certainly, but also because of carefully chosen involvement in broader cultural events and strategic business decisions to expand into traditionally non-music commercial enterprises.

Their engagement has been fiscally and philanthropically motivated. By traveling the globe several times, the band has crossed cultural and socioeconomic lines and reached people of different generations and remote geographic locations.

Despite having written some of the most popular songs in American culture, Bon Jovi has not been inducted into the Rock and Roll Hall of Fame since becoming eligible in 2009. Being rejected by the "Hall" will continue to be a thorn in Bon Jovi's side, but it has not been a surprise to the band. They have dealt with nonacceptance by music critics and industry professionals their whole career. Gaining entry to the Hall will most likely require a marketing campaign of some type but will eventually happen.

Jon Bon Jovi has not been a typical lead singer, though in many ways he fits the stereotype of good-looking, charismatic, and energetic. He is a more complex man than one would think at first glance. His leadership has kept the Bon Jovi enterprise running for decades; he explored another career in acting because he likes challenges; and, most importantly, he has created a philanthropic foundation that is providing real, tangible help. The self-described "quarterback" of the Bon Jovi team is now a player in the American political arena.

A large part of the appeal of Jon Bon Jovi to women is the fact that he is married to his first wife. In the entertainment industry this is the exception, not the rule. Women like the fact that he is a good husband and father, but there is reason to think that he has had his struggles like the rest of us. In a 1998 *Movieline* interview, during a discussion about fidelity in marriage, Jon said, "The only thing I like more than my wife is my money." He went on to say he would not be losing any of his money to "her and her lawyers." He immediately concedes "there's going to be hell to pay for that line."[3] In contrast, in an interview more than ten years later, Jon comes across with more acumen and sensitivity: "I am wise enough to realize that women are much smarter than any man, and that women control the world." When the interviewer goes on to ask him if he is a feminist he replies, "Yeah! Yeah! And . . . this idea that the pay scale is unequal is beyond my comprehension. Every man knows, and if he doesn't say it, he's a liar . . . that they get their wisdom from their mother, their wife and their daughters."[4] This is the anti–rock star speaking.

Jon Bon Jovi will have the last word as to what Bon Jovi's legacy will be. It may not be the music. Jon has the ability to inspire people. When speaking to a crowd about homelessness in America, he has received spontaneous and genuine applause. He has strong feelings about community service and will most likely continue to accomplish service projects through his foundation. He has said that he would like to "make volunteerism the new black," and he is on his way to doing it.

The man and the band Bon Jovi have always done things their own way. Building on their Jersey roots and learning from the Asbury Park musicians of the '70s and '80s, they have created a discography of records that are now enmeshed in American culture. There is no greater testament to Bon Jovi than fans including their songs as part of the soundtrack of their lives.

NOTES

1. AN AMERICAN BAND

1. Forum discussion, http://www.bonjovi.com/
2. Toby Goldstein, "Bon Jovi Says: Everybody in the Pool," *Creem*, January 1987: 40.
3. Gary Wien, *Beyond the Palace* (Canada: Trafford Publishing, 2003), 81.
4. Christa Titus, "An MTV Moment," *Billboard*, 20 November 1984: 32.
5. Titus, "An MTV Moment," 32.
6. Forum discussion, http://www.bonjovi.com/
7. John Neilson, "Freshening the Air with Bon Jovi," *Creem*, June 1985: 64.
8. Emily Yoffe, "Music to the Eyes," *The Washington Post Magazine*, June 1984: 15.
9. Neilson, "Freshening the Air with Bon Jovi," 42.
10. Ken Tucker, "The Scorpions at the Spectrum," *Philadephia Inquirer*, June 1984: 30.
11. Mick Wall, *All Night Long: The True Story of Bon Jovi* (London: Omnibus Press, 1995), 22.
12. Wall, *All Night Long*, 22.
13. Joe Sasfy, "Bon Jovi: Tempered Heavy Metal," *Washington Post*, 16 March 1984.
14. "1984 Arts/Entertainment The Year in Review," *Morning Call*, 30 December 1984.
15. Tucker, "The Scorpions at the Spectrum."
16. Terry Atkinson, "Scorpions' Feat: Fans Stay on Their Feet," *Los Angeles Times*, 26 April 1984.

17. Len Righi, "Hot Air Balloons Ascend the Chart," *Morning Call*, 25 May 1985.

2. THE SONGS

1. Redbeard, *In the Studio*, radio interview, 17 August 2011.
2. Redbeard, *In the Studio*.
3. Redbeard, *In the Studio*.
4. Redbeard, *In the Studio*.
5. Jon Pareles, "Pop, Cute, Fit, and Leather-Clad," *New York Times*, 18 March 1989.
6. "Jersey Hero," *P Magazine*, 10 September 2002.
7. Glen Osrin, http://www.examiner.com, 20 August 2010.
8. Live poll taken in 2008, 2010.
9. Redbeard, *In the Studio*.
10. Redbeard, *In the Studio*.
11. Redbeard, *In the Studio*.
12. Nathan Thornburgh, "10 Questions for Jon Bon Jovi," http://www.time.com/, 25 July 2007.
13. Christa Titus, "Always a Hard-Working Band," *Billboard*, 20 November 1984.
14. David Browne, "Review," *Entertainment Weekly*, 6 September 1991, http://www.ew.com/
15. http://www.davidbryan.com/
16. Toby Goldstein, "Bon Jovi Says: Everybody in the Pool," *Creem*, January 1987.

3. MTV'S BAND FOR A GENERATION

1. http://www.mtv.com/
2. Craig Marks and Rob Tannenbaum, *I Want My MTV: The Uncensored Story of the Music Video Revolution* (New York: Dutton, 2011), 558.
3. Marks and Tannenbaum, *I Want My MTV*, 94.
4. Marks and Tannenbaum, *I Want My MTV*, 335.
5. Marks and Tannenbaum, *I Want My MTV*, 240.
6. Marks and Tannenbaum, *I Want My MTV*, 345.
7. Karen Schoemer, "Recordings View: Bon Jovi's New Sound: Lean, Tough, Uneasy," *New York Times*, 15 November 1992: 30.

8. Marks and Tannenbaum, *I Want My MTV*, 558.

9. Marks and Tannenbaum, *I Want My MTV*, 333.

10. Marks and Tannenbaum, *I Want My MTV*, 333.

11. Marks and Tannenbaum, *I Want My MTV*, 445.

12. Marks and Tannenbaum, *I Want My MTV*, 448.

13. David Cobb Craig and Chris Coats, "Rock Climbers," *People* (vol. 56, no. 16), 15 October 2001.

14. Toby Goldstein, "Bon Jovi Says: Everybody in the Pool," *Creem*, January 1987.

15. Marks and Tannenbaum, *I Want My MTV*, 333.

16. Christa Titus, "An MTV Moment," *Billboard*, 20 November 1984: 32.

17. Marks and Tannenbaum, *I Want My MTV*, 335.

18. Marks and Tannenbaum, *I Want My MTV*, 313.

19. http://www.mtv.com/

20. Marks and Tannenbaum, *I Want My MTV*, 16.

21. Marks and Tannenbaum, *I Want My MTV*, 16.

22. Steven Holden, "Music Video Leaves Its Mark on the Film 'Footloose,'" *New York Times*, 4 March 1984.

4. EXCESS AND SOBRIETY

1. http://www.abcnews.com/

2. Joe Bosso, "Sammy Hagar Blames Tequila for Zeppelin Comment," http://www.musicradar.com/, 2008.

3. http://www.rocknewsdesk.com/, 8 March 2011.

4. Craig Marks and Rob Tannenbaum, *I Want My MTV: The Uncensored Story of the Music Video Revolution* (New York: Dutton, 2011), 270.

5. Marks and Tannenbaum, *I Want My MTV*, 163.

6. Marks and Tannenbaum, *I Want My MTV*, 162.

7. Marks and Tannenbaum, *I Want My MTV*, 501.

8. Tim Nudd, "Jon Bon Jovi Admits He's Been 'No Saint,'" *People*, 15 October 2007.

9. Tommy Lee et al., *Mötley Crüe: The Dirt: Confessions of the World's Most Notorious Rock Band* (New York: HarperCollins Publishers, Inc., 2002), 224–27.

10. "Oprah's Master Class with Jon Bon Jovi," http://www.oprah.com/, 25 March 2012.

11. Lee et al., *Mötley Crüe: The Dirt*, 224–27.

12. "Oprah's Master Class with Jon Bon Jovi."

13. *When We Were Beautiful*, documentary film DVD (Radical Media, 2009).

14. *When We Were Beautiful*.

15. *When We Were Beautiful*.

5. CROSS-COMMERCIALISM AS A SURVIVAL TOOL

1. Advil, television commercial, 2012.

2. Jennifer Rooney, "The Story behind Jon Bon Jovi's First Endorsement in His 30-Year Career," *CMO Network*, 9 December 2011.

3. http://www.rollingstone.com/

4. *When We Were Beautiful*, documentary film DVD (Radical Media, 2009).

5. Simon Perry, "Rihanna 'Lives on a Prayer' with Bon Jovi in Madrid," *People*, 7 November 2010.

6. *When We Were Beautiful*.

7. *When We Were Beautiful*.

8. *When We Were Beautiful*.

9. *When We Were Beautiful*.

10. David W. Chen, "Worth Noting, Turning to Bon Jovi to Lure Tourists," *New York Times*, 16 April 2006.

11. Bon Jovi, "You Give Love a Bad Name," *Slippery When Wet* (Mercury, 1986).

12. *When We Were Beautiful*.

13. http://www.monmouth.edu/

14. Julia Neel, "White Trash Beautiful," http://www.vogue.uk.com/news/, 23 June 2010.

15. Adam Tschorn, "Richie Sambora and Nikki Lund to Duet on the Runway," http://www.latimes.com/, 19 March 2010.

6. THE GENDER DIVIDE?

1. *When We Were Beautiful*, documentary film DVD (Radical Media, 2009).

2. Redbeard, *In the Studio*, radio interview, 17 August 2011.

3. Redbeard, *In the Studio*.

4. Redbeard, *In the Studio*.

5. Redbeard, *In the Studio*.

6. Redbeard, *In the Studio*.

7. Personal interview with Ed Jankowski, 2012.

8. Personal interview with Ed Jankowski.

9. Tom Gliatto, "Local Boy Makes Good," *People* (vol. 58, no. 22), 25 November 2002.

10. Erik Hedegaard, "Profile of a Rock Star: Jon Bon Jovi Is More Complicated than You Think," *Men's Health*, 20 June 2007.

11. Sia Michel, "Bon Jovi Comes Home to New Jersey, with Sound and Hair Still Big," *New York Times*, 20 July 2006.

12. Hedegaard, "Profile of a Rock Star."

13. Tiffany McGee, "Jon Bon Jovi Answers Your Questions," *People* (vol. 68, no. 2), 9 July 2007.

14. Gliatto, "Local Boy Makes Good."

15. Gliatto, "Local Boy Makes Good."

16. "No Don Juan: Jon Bon Jovi Marries His High School Sweetheart in a Vegas Chapel," *People* (vol. 31, no. 20), 22 May 1989.

17. Live poll conducted in 2010, 2011, 2012.

18. Personal interview with Ed Jankowski.

19. Kevin Cahillane, "Adolescent Angst: When the Karate Kid Fell for Jon Bon Jovi," *New York Times*, 12 December 2004.

20. *When We Were Beautiful*.

7. THE BON JOVI BRAND

1. Jerry McLaughlin, "The Power of Brand Building," http://www.forbes.com/, 8 December 2011.

2. "Old Rockers Who Have Turned Into Top Business People," http://www.forbes.com/, 24 August 2011.

3. Mary Campbell, "Bon Jovi Finally Gets It Right," *South Florida Sun Sentinel*, 13 February 1987.

4. Ben Sisario, "Full Album Sales Showed a Little Growth in 2011," http://www.latimes.com/, 4 January 2012.

5. David Goldman, "Music's Last Decade: Sales Cut in Half," http://www.cnnmoney.com/, 3 February 2010.

6. Ray Waddell, "Now and Forever," *Billboard*, 22 October 2011: 15.

7. http://www.bonjovi.com/

8. Ray Waddell, "Keeping the Faith," *Billboard* (vol. 122, no. 50), 2010: 63–70.

9. Lauren Musacchio, "Jon Bon Jovi Partners with Avon for 'Unplugged' Fragrances," http://www.rollingstone.com/, 2 July 2012.

10. Waddell, "Now and Forever," 22.

11. Polly Vernon, "I'm Overweight, Drinking Too Much. Bored to Tears," *Observer*, 30 October 2010.

12. Cameron Adams, "Bon Jovi Live Melbourne Concert," *Herald Sun*, 11 December 2010.

13. Redbeard, *In the Studio*, radio interview, 17 August 2011.

14. Waddell, "Keeping the Faith," 63–70.

15. Waddell, "Keeping the Faith," 63–70.

16. Jerry Shriver, "Bon Jovi Getting Down to Business as a Band and Brand," *USA Today*, 13 November 2009.

17. *When We Were Beautiful*, documentary film DVD (Radical Media, 2009).

18. http://www.bonjovi.com/

19. "Bon Jovi Unveils Clips from New Documentary," *Billboard Magazine*, 25 September 2008.

20. Waddell, "Keeping the Faith," 63–70.

8. PHILANTHROPY—BON JOVI'S OTHER LEGACY

1. Jon Widerhorn, "Bon Jovi Put Post-9/11 Faith, Hope, Energy into *Bounce*," http://www.mtv.com/, 12 September 2002.

2. http://www.unsolved.com/

3. *Larry King Live*, television interview, 9 December 2010.

4. Ray Waddell, "Keeping the Faith," *Billboard* (vol. 122, no. 50), 2010: 63–70.

5. Adam Hanft, "Soul Proprietor: Jon Bon Jovi," *Inc. Magazine*, 1 July 2004.

6. http://www.jbjsoulfoundation.com/

7. "Barbara Bush Calls Evacuees Better Off," *New York Times*, 7 September 2005.

8. Jerry Shriver, "Bon Jovi Getting Down to Business as a Band and Brand," *USA Today*, 13 November 2009.

9. Gene Johnson, "Bon Jovi Tour Doubles as Homeless Research Mission," Associated Press, 26 February 2010.

10. "Bon Jovi Opens Charitable Pay-What-You-Can Restaurant in New Jersey," http://www.huffingtonpost.com/

11. http://www.jbjsoulkitchen.com/

12. Polly Vernon, "I'm Overweight, Drinking Too Much. Bored to Tears," *Observer*, 30 October 2010.

13. http://www.whitehouse.com/

14. Kevin M. Ryan, "Up Close with Jon Bon Jovi: 'Each of Us Has the Power to Effect Change. You Needn't Be a Rock Star,'" http://www.huffingtonpost.com/

15. "Jon Bon Jovi Youth 'Listening Tour' Comes to Newark, New Jersey," CBS New York, 6 June 2011.

16. "Jon Bon Jovi Youth 'Listening Tour' Comes to Newark, New Jersey."

17. National Conference of Volunteering and Service, 30 June 2009.

18. *Larry King Live*.

19. *Person to Person*, television interview, CBS News, 8 February 2012.

EPILOGUE

1. Steve Kroft, "Bon Jovi's Opening Act," CBS News, 18 May 2008.

2. David Ling, "Bassist's Instinct," *RAW Magazine* (no. 154), 1994.

3. Martha Frankel, "Jon Bon Jovi: Music to the Eyes," *Movieline*, 1 February 1998.

4. Polly Vernon, "I'm Overweight, Drinking Too Much. Bored to Tears," *Observer* 30 October 2010.

WORKS CITED

"1984 Arts/Entertainment The Year in Review." *Morning Call* 30 December 1984. Print.

http://www.abcnews.com/. Web.

Adams, Cameron. "Bon Jovi Live Melbourne Concert." *Herald Sun* 11 December 2010. Print.

Advil. Television Commercial. 2012.

Atkinson, Terry. "Scorpions' Feat: Fans Stay on Their Feet." *Los Angeles Times* 26 April 1984. Print.

"Barbara Bush Calls Evacuees Better Off." *New York Times* 7 September 2005. Print.

http://www.billboard.com/. 29 April 2011: n. pag. Web.

http://www.bonjovi.com/. Web.

"Bon Jovi Backstage at iHeartRadio Music Festival." http://www.billboard.com/. n. pag. Web.

"Bon Jovi: Because We Can—The Tour." http://www.financialpost.com/. 25 October 2010: n. pag. Web.

"Bon Jovi DC Show Goes Wireless." http://www.billboard.com/. n. pag. Web.

"Bon Jovi Opens Charitable Pay-What-You-Can Restaurant in New Jersey." http://www.huffingtonpost.com/. n. pag. Web.

"Bon Jovi Tops the 2010 Tour List." http://www.latimes.com/. 28 December 2010: n. pag. Web.

"Bon Jovi Unveils Clips from New Documentary." http://www.billboard.com/. 25 September 2008. n. pag. Web.

Bon Jovi. "You Give Love a Bad Name." *Slippery When Wet*. Mercury, 1986. CD.

Bosso, Joe. "Sammy Hagar Blames Tequila for Zeppelin Comment." http://www.musicradar.com/ 2008: n. pag. Web.

Bowler, Dave and Dray, Bryan. *Bon Jovi: Runaway*. London: Boxtree Limited London, 1995. Print.

Bozzett, Rich. *Sex, Drugs and Bon Jovi (1983–1989)*. Blumberg Corporate Services, 2010. Print.

Browne, David. "Review." *Entertainment Weekly* 6 September 1991. Print.

Cahillane, Kevin. "Adolescent Angst: When the Karate Kid Fell for Jon Bon Jovi." *New York Times* 12 December 2004. Print.

Campbell, Mary. "Bon Jovi Finally Gets It Right." *South Florida Sun Sentinel* 13 February 1987. Print.

http://www.center4research.org/. Web.

Chen, David W. "Worth Noting, Turning to Bon Jovi to Lure Tourists." *New York Times* 16 April 2006. Print.

Chiu, Alexis. "Heather Locklear and Richie Sambora's Divorce Finalized." *People* 11 April 2007. Print.

Connelly, Albie. "Charity Begins at Home with Alliance of Neighbors." *Atlanticville* 25 October 2001. Print.

http://www.coty.com/. Web.

Craig, David Cobb and Coats, Chris. "Fan Wins Singer's House." *People* 2001. Print.

Daunt, Tina. "Obama Joins Bill Clinton, Jon Bon Jovi at Three New York Fundraisers." http://www.freerepublic.com/. 4 June 2012: n. pag. Web.

Davalos, Adriana. "White Trash Beautiful Fashion Show Review." Splash Magazine, http://www.lasplash.com. n. dat., n. pag. Web.

http://www.davidbryan.com/. Web.

http://www.ew.com/. Web.

Forum discussion. http://www.bonjovi.com/. Web.

Frankel, Martha. "Jon Bon Jovi: Music to the Eyes." *Movieline* 1 February 1998. Print.

"Fund-Raiser with Barack Obama and Jon Bon Jovi Carries High Price Tag." http://www.nj.com/. 14 September 2008: n. pag. Web.

Gliatto, Tom. "Local Boy Makes Good." *People* 25 November 2002. Print.

Goldman, David. "Music's Last Decade: Sales Cut in Half." http://www.cnnmoney.com/. 3 February 2010: n. pag. Web.

Goldstein, Toby. "Bon Jovi Says: Everybody in the Pool." *Creem* January 1987: 38–41. Print.

Hanft, Adam. "Soul Proprietor: Jon Bon Jovi." *Inc. Magazine* 1 July 2004. Print.

Hedegaard, Erik. "Profile of a Rock Star: Jon Bon Jovi Is More Complicated than You Think." *Men's Health* 20 June 2007. Print.

Holden, Steven. "Music Video Leaves Its Mark on the Film 'Footloose.'" *New York Times* 4 March 1984. Print.

Hudak, Joseph. "Chris Daughtry Opens Up about Idol, Bon Jovi, and His Grammy Noms." *TV Guide* 8 February 2008. Print.

http://www.huffingtonpost.com/. Web.

Jackson, Laura. *Jon Bon Jovi*. New York: Kensington Publishing Corporation, 2003. Print.

Jan, Ramona. *Bon Jovi*. New York: Paperjacks, 1988. Print.

Jankowski, Ed. Personal Interview.

http://www.jbjsoulfoundation.com/. 2012. Web.

"Jersey Hero." *P Magazine* 10 September 2002. Print.

"Jimmy Buffett, 62, Is Cashing In on Margaritaville." http://www.money.usnews.com/. 6 February 2009: n. pag. Web.

Johnson, Gene. "Bon Jovi Tour Doubles as Homeless Research Mission." Associated Press 26 February 2010. Print.

"Jon Bon Jovi Youth 'Listening Tour' Comes to Newark, New Jersey." *CBS New York* 6 June 2011. Print.

Kroft, Steve. "Bon Jovi's Opening Act." CBS News 18 May 2008. Television Show. http://www.lasplash.com/. Web.

Larry King Live. 9 December 2010. Television Interview.

Lee, Ken. "Heather Locklear Arrested for Hit-and-Run." *People* 22 April 2010. Print.

Lee, Tommy; Mars, Mick; Neil, Vince; Sixx, Nikki; and Strauss, Neil. *Mötley Crüe: The Dirt: Confessions of the World's Most Notorious Rock Band.* New York: HarperCollins Publishers, Inc., 2002. Print.

Library of Congress. http://www.loc.gov/. Web.

Ling, David. "Bassist's Instinct." *RAW Magazine* 1994. Print.

Maris, David. "Bon Jovi's Next Hit Could Be an App for the Homeless." http://www.forbes.com/. n. pag. Web.

Marks, Craig and Tannenbaum, Rob. *I Want My MTV: The Uncensored Story of the Music Video Revolution.* New York: Dutton, 2011. Print.

McGee, Tiffany. "Jon Bon Jovi Answers Your Questions." *People* 9 July 2007. Print.

McLaughlin, Jerry. "The Power of Brand Building." http://www.forbes.com/. 8 December 2011: n. pag. Web.

Michel, Sia. "Bon Jovi Comes Home to New Jersey, with Sound and Hair Still Big." *New York Times* 20 July 2006. Print.

http://www.monmouth.edu/. Web.

http://www.mtv.com/. Web.

Musacchio, Lauren. "Jon Bon Jovi Partners with Avon for 'Unplugged' Fragrances." http://www.rollingstone.com/. 2 July 2012: n. pag. Web.

National Conference of Volunteering and Service. http://www.youtube.com/. 30 June 2009. n. pag. Web.

"NBC Names Jon Bon Jovi Artist in Residence." *New York Times* 15 October 2009. Print.

"NBC's NFL Kickoff 2011: Back to Football with Jon Bon Jovi." http://www.rbr.com/. 8 September 2011: n. pag. Web.

Neel, Julia. "White Trash Beautiful." http://www.vogue.uk.com/news/. 23 June 2010: n. pag. Web.

Neilson, John. "Freshening the Air with Bon Jovi." *Creem* June 1985: 64. Print.

"No Don Juan: Jon Bon Jovi Marries His High School Sweetheart in a Vegas Chapel." *People* 22 May 1989. Print.

http://www.northernchildren.org/. Web.

Nudd, Tim. "Jon Bon Jovi Admits He's Been 'No Saint.'" *People* 15 October 2007. Print.

"Old Rockers Who Have Turned Into Top Business People." http://www.forbes.com/. 24 August 2011: n. pag. Web.

"Oprah's Master Class with Jon Bon Jovi." http://www.oprah.com/. 25 March 2012: n. pag. Web.

Osrin, Glen. http://www.examiner.com. 20 August 2010: n. pag. Web.

Pareles, Jon. "Pop, Cute, Fit, and Leather-Clad." *New York Times* 18 March 1989. Print.

http://www.people.com/. 29 March 2008: n. pag. Web.

"Performers Should Speak Out against Drugs." *Billboard* 1986: 9. Web.

Perry, Simon. "Rihanna 'Lives on a Prayer' with Bon Jovi in Madrid." *People* 7 November 2010. Print.

Person to Person. CBS News 8 February 2012. Television Interview.

Popson, Tom. "Faking Out Fans in Japan: A Lesson from Bon Jovi." *Chicago Tribune* September 1985. Print.

Press Office. http://www.whitehouse.gov/. 14 December 2010. Web.

Redbeard. "In the Studio." 17 August 2011. Radio Interview.

Righi, Len. "Hot Air Balloons Ascend the Chart." *Morning Call* 25 May 1985. Print.

http://www.rocknewsdesk.com/. 8 March 2011: n. pag. Web.

"Rock Stars Make Peace Prize List." *BBC News* 24 February 2006. Print.

http://www.rollingstone.com/. Web.

Rooney, Jennifer. "The Story behind Jon Bon Jovi's First Endorsement in His 30-Year Career." *CMO Network* 9 December 2011. Print.

Ryan, Kevin M. "Up Close with Jon Bon Jovi: 'Each of Us Has the Power to Effect Change. You Needn't Be a Rock Star.'" http://www.huffingtonpost.com/. n. pag. Web.

Sasfy, Joe. "Bon Jovi: Tempered Heavy Metal." *Washington Post* 16 March 1984. Print.

Saul, Michael. "JBJ to Headline Fund-Raiser for Hillary Clinton's Campaign Debt." http://www.nydailynews.com/. 2 January 2009: n. pag. Web.

Schoemer, Karen. "Recordings View: Bon Jovi's New Sound: Lean, Tough, Uneasy." *New York Times* 15 November 1992: 30. Print.

Serjeant, Jill. "Actress Heather Locklear in Hospital after 911 Call." http://www.reuters.com/. 12 January 2012: n. pag. Web.

http://www.serve.gov/. Web.

http://www.servicenation.com/. Web.

Shriver, Jerry. "Bon Jovi Getting Down to Business as a Band and Brand." *USA Today* 13 November 2009. Print.

Sisario, Ben. "Full Album Sales Showed a Little Growth in 2011." http://www.latimes.com/. 4 January 2012: n. pag. Web.

Thornburgh, Nathan. "10 Questions for Jon Bon Jovi." http://www.time.com/. 25 July 2007: n. pag. Web.

Titus, Christa. "Always a Hard-Working Band." *Billboard* 20 November 1984. Print.

———. "An MTV Moment." *Billboard* 20 November 1984: 32. Print.

Tschorn, Adam. "Richie Sambora and Nikki Lund to Duet on the Runway." http://www.latimes.com/. 19 March 2010: n. pag. Web.

Tucker, Ken. "The Scorpions at the Spectrum." *Philadephia Inquirer* June 1984: 30. Print.

http://www.unsolved.com/. Web.

Van Embden, Edward. "Pasta with a Side of Bon Jovi." *Red Bank-Shrewsbury Patch* 6 June 2012. Print.

Vena, Jocelyn. "'A Change Is Gonna Come' Takes on New Meaning at Inaugural Concert." http://www.mtv.com/. 18 January 2009: n. pag. Web.

Vernon, Polly. "I'm Overweight, Drinking Too Much. Bored to Tears." *Observer* 30 October 2010. Print.

Waddell, Ray. "Now and Forever." *Billboard* 22 October 2011: 15–19. Print.

———. "Keeping the Faith." *Billboard* 2010: 63–70. Print.

Wall, Mick. *All Night Long: The True Story of Bon Jovi*. London: Omnibus Press, 1995. Print.

When We Were Beautiful. Documentary Film DVD. Radical Media, 2009.

http://www.whitehouse.com/. Web.

Widerhorn, Jon. "Bon Jovi Put Post-9/11 Faith, Hope, Energy into *Bounce*." http://www.mtv.com/. 12 September 2002: n. pag. Web.

———. "Concert for New York City Raises Over $30 Million." http://www.mtv.com/. 2 November 2001: n. pag. Web.

Wien, Gary. *Beyond the Palace*. Canada: Trafford Publishing, 2003. Print.

Yoffe, Emily. "Music to the Eyes." *The Washington Post Magazine* June 1984: 15. Print.

BON JOVI ALBUMS

Bon Jovi (21 January 1984), Album, Worldwide Release, Mercury Records. Jon Bon Jovi's original song, "Runaway," is the clear breakout single from the album. While the lyrics reflect the interests of men in their early twenties, the music packs a punch as an example of solid Jersey rock.

7800° Fahrenheit (12 April 1985), Album, Worldwide Release, Mercury Records. Bon Jovi's second album does not have the freedom and energy of the first album or the catchy hits of the third album, yet singles "In and Out of Love" and "Only Lonely" made the Billboard 100.

Slippery When Wet (18 August 1986), Album, Worldwide Release, Mercury Records. The band's most successful album and one of the most loved rock albums of all time. The singles "Livin' on a Prayer" and "Wanted Dead or Alive" helped to define the '80s and Music Television (MTV).

New Jersey (13 September 1988), Album, Worldwide Release, Polygram Records. The follow-up album to *Slippery* that exceeded all expectations; representative hits include "Born to Be My Baby," "Bad Medicine," and "I'll Be There for You." The music contains classic riffs, catchy melodies, and slick production values.

Keep the Faith (3 November 1992), Album, Worldwide Release, Mercury Records. The band experiments musically by utilizing blues and hard rock in tunes like "Dry County," "If I Was Your Mother," "Little Bit of Soul," and "Fear." The title single, "Keep the Faith," is the most successful track, and "Bed of Roses" remains a concert ballad staple for the band.

Cross Road: Greatest Hits (10 October 1994), Album, Worldwide Release, Island/Mercury. Bon Jovi's first of several greatest hits albums. The two newly written tracks on the album are the frequently performed "Someday I'll Be Saturday Night" and "Always."

These Days (27 June 1995), Album, Worldwide Release, Mercury Records. A decidedly more mature Bon Jovi is evident on the album as their lyrics explore heavier themes of faith, God, and the meaning of life. The band takes risks on songs like "Something to Believe In" and "Damned." "Hearts Breaking Even" is clearly influenced by Aerosmith's "Cryin'."

Crush (13 June 2000), Album, Worldwide Release, Island Def Jam. Crush is one of Bon Jovi's most successful albums in the second half of their career. "It's My Life" is the breakout single off the record that endeared the group to a newer, younger audience.

Tokyo Road: Best of Bon Jovi (28 March 2001), Album, Worldwide Release, Universal Japan. A compilation album exclusively released in Japan.

One Wild Night Live 1985–2001 (22 May 2001), Album, Worldwide Release, Island. The album is a compilation of the band's biggest hits and a cover of a Neil Young song.

Bounce (8 October 2002), Album, Worldwide Release, Island Def Jam. *Bounce* is the reflection of a cleaner, leaner, and no-nonsense Bon Jovi. "Undivided" is a clear response to 9/11 and has an uplifting and defiant feel.

The Left Feels Right: Greatest Hits with a Twist (4 November 2003), Album, Worldwide Release, Island. As the title suggests, this album is often left of center, and not always in a good way. Fans may or may not appreciate the new interpretations of classic Bon Jovi hits that make up this record.

100,000 Bon Jovi Fans Can't Be Wrong (16 November 2004), Boxed Set, Worldwide Release, Island Def Jam. A large compilation album with over fifty unreleased tracks and songs reminiscent of artists like Tina Turner ("Shut Up and Kiss Me") and the Rolling Stones ("Too Much of a Good Thing"). True fans will appreciate Richie Sambora's vocal solo turn on "If I Can't Have Your Love" and drummer Tico Torres's on "Only in My Dreams."

Have a Nice Day (20 September 2005), Album, Worldwide Release, Island Def Jam. "Have a Nice Day," "Story of My Life," and "Last Cigarette" establish a fresh musical style for the band; "Who Says You Can't Go Home" is the album's breakout song.

Lost Highway (8 June 2007), Album, Worldwide Release, Island/Mercury. Recorded with an eclectic group of musicians in Nashville, *Lost Highway* is a country-influenced rock record that brings out thoughtful and effective vocals from Jon Bon Jovi. Huge hits off the first Bon Jovi record to debut at number one on the Billboard chart include "We Got It Goin' On" and "Who Says You Can't Go Home," a duet with Jennifer Nettles.

The Circle (10 November 2009), Album, North American Release, Island Def Jam. *The Circle* is a return to big stadium rock anthems like "We Weren't Born to Follow" and "Work for the Working Man." Fans will appreciate that Bon Jovi has circled back to their rock roots after the experimental, country-infused previous album.

Greatest Hits: The Ultimate Collection (9 November 2010), Album, North American Release, Island Def Jam. A comprehensive greatest hits collection that spans twenty-five years and contains most of the commercially successful songs by the band. This album is a must-have for fans.

What About Now? (8 March 2013), Album, Worldwide Release, Island Def Jam. The newest Bon Jovi album takes the band in a new musical direction. The new stadium anthem "That's What the Water Made Me" is a standout, as are two retro ballads, "Amen" and "The Fighter."

INDEX

ABOUT THE AUTHOR

Margaret Olson is an educator, musician, and writer who has been livin' on a prayer since the mid-1980s. She has been on the music faculty at the University of Tennessee, Morgan State University, and Georgetown University. She has taught music programs for the Washington National Opera Institute, Peabody Conservatory and Preparatory, and the Wolf Trap Foundation, among others. She has written extensively about music topics and been published in several national academic journals. She is the author of *The Solo Singer in the Choral Setting*. She holds a doctor of musical arts degree from the University of Iowa. Her mentors include Geraldine Cate, Joel Adams, William P. Carroll, Nancy L. Walker, Leon Major, Carroll Gonzo, Richard Sjoerdsma, Ingo Titze, Sally Stunkel, and Shirley Basfield Dunlap. This is her first book on a popular music subject.

DATE			